The Satterfield Flyer

Adventures of a Country Veterinarian and Newspaper Editor

in Sullivan County, Pennsylvania

*6/8/15*

*To charlie*

*best regards*

*TW Shoemaker*

*"Doc"*

**Dr. T.W. Shoemaker**

Edited by Judith Terry Smith

ISBN: 978-1-4951-4149-2

# Table of Contents

## Section 1: Doc and Stevie Shoemaker Come to Sullivan County, PA and Co-publish *The Sullivan Review*

## Section 2: Dushore's Beginnings, Postcards from the 1890s On

## Section 3: Animal Patients and Farm Calls

## Section 4: The Veterinary Office

## Section 5: Dairy Industry in Sullivan County

## Section 6: Dushore Borough and Around the County

## Section 7: Outdoors in the Endless Mountains

## Section 8: Sullivan County Railroads, Trolleys and Doc's Rail Car

## Section 9: Recollections

## List of images

## Section 1: Doc and Stevie Shoemaker Come to Sullivan County, PA and Co-publish *The Sullivan Review*

## Section 2: Dushore's Beginnings, Postcards from the 1890s on

## Section 3: Animal Patients and Farm Calls

## Section 4: The Veterinary Office

## Section 5: Dairy Industry in Sullivan County

## Section 6: Dushore Borough and Around the County

## Section 7: Outdoors in the Endless Mountains

## Section 8: Sullivan County Railroads, Trolleys and Doc's Rail Car

## Section 9: Recollections

# Dedication

"Stevie"
Stefana (Hoyniak) Shoemaker and Layla
January 9, 2008

# Forward

When people ask where I am from, the reflex answer is Sullivan County, Pennsylvania. Not a city or town, but a whole county, a state of mind. Like all places in the realm of Americana, the county has gone through its changes. But this place is unique (I like to think), and changes, when they happen, are absorbed and dealt with in a decidedly Sullivan County way. It is one of those places where, when you are here, the outside world and it's frenetic pace and attitudes seem irrelevant. It is fitting that this special place is the setting for the following collection of stories, pictures, and recollections.

As a young man fighting for my academic life in veterinary school, I looked for any source of inspiration and encouragement I could on the way to graduation. The main form of this inspiration came from "Grandpa Doc," and was received with some regularity. These short letters, which were always on the back of a piece of junk mail, scrap paper, or invoice, read like an unofficial version of the "Satterfield Flyer," always handwritten, with the place and date from where and when the letters were sent (usually Dushore, PA) in distinctive scrawled pen strokes. They were written, I presume, on his lunch break or between photo shoots for the paper or on the operating table after the morning surgeries were done. As my time through school and career progressed, and with it, my experiences, the letters became more veterinary related. As we shared experiences comparing a 1950 graduate to a 2010 graduate, many cases were surprisingly similar and many outcomes the same despite 60 years of new medicine and technology. At its core, the veterinary business is a people business as much as it is about medicine, surgery, and science. That is one of the reasons that Doc's adventures make such memorable stories; it would be hard to make up some of the characters and scenarios that have been part of his Sullivan County experience.

Tom Shoemaker, DVM
Sunset Beach, NC

# Introduction

When Doc and Stevie Shoemaker bought the weekly newspaper, *The Sullivan Review*, they also bought into the history and culture of Sullivan County, a largely wooded area in the Endless Mountains of northeastern Pennsylvania.

Doc has always had a special interest in preserving history, whether through writing and photography or support of local historical societies and museums. His collections of postcards, posters, letters, railroad memorabilia and photographs provide an authentic look at earlier times, and the hard work of farming and lumbering before modern conveniences. We hope you enjoy remembering or learning about those earlier times.

Sullivan County's "development" over the years depended on two companies, the Lehigh Valley and the Williamsport and North Branch (W&NB) Railroads, both of which provided passenger and freight service to the area. The Lehigh Valley ran from Muncy, in Lycoming County, to Towanda, in Bradford County, but the W&NB ended at Satterfield, a tiny settlement about four miles south of Dushore in Cherry Township.

People often ask how Doc's occasional columns in *The Sullivan Review* came to be called "The Satterfield Flyer." With his love of railroads and the need for a moniker, he liked the name of the daily train, shown here in a photograph by his friend George M. Hart, director of the Railroad Museum of Pennsylvania at Strasburg, Lancaster County, PA. Today there is no

The Satterfield Flyer, Satterfield Station, and photographer George M. Hart's Willys Knight auto, 1939.

trace of the train, its tracks or the station, which was named for John Satterfield, one of the owners of the W&NB who raised funds to complete the railroad. Service to Satterfield began in September 1893 and ended in 1937 (Taber, 1969).

The columns are first person accounts of rural life in the decades before telephones were common in many homes, let alone cell phones and the Internet. Farmers and those interested in veterinary medicine will note the transition from observational diagnoses to the test-based procedures of present-day examinations. Doc relates easily to local farmers, their families and pet owners ("Hound Dog Duke"), as well as visitors ("City Dog"). He has a magic touch for photographing large litters of wiggily puppies brought to the vet office for shots. He is so trusted by his animal patients that once a runaway horse showed up at the office. Doc tied it to a tree while he called around to find the owner, who was up on the mountain cutting logs (*The Sullivan Review*, August 11, 2010).

Photographs and stories from Doc's more than 60 years as a country veterinarian were used for The Sully's signature large image on page 1 of the paper, and for more than 200 columns. Almost 100 of the columns, most describing Sullivan County, are included here. Images are mainly by Doc except as noted, or from the published and unpublished photographs in his private collection and the archives of *The Sullivan Review*. Most of the photographs were not taken at the time the articles were written, but they convey the timeless beauty of rural scenes and the interesting people of Sullivan County.

Judith Terry Smith, editor
Arlington, VA

# Section
# 1

*Doc and Stevie Shoemaker Come*
*to Sullivan County, PA and*
*Co-Publish The Sullivan Review*

van Revi

The Sullivan Review building, originally a firehouse, opposite the Dushore Monument. The Shoemakers purchased the building in 1972.

## Reflections on 40 Years at The Sully

Forty years ago when we assumed ownership of *The Sullivan Review*, our first issue was published on September 2, 1966. Little did we know that a weekly newspaper would be a 24-hours a day, 7 days a week, proposition. Like a herd of dairy cattle, always something to do, every day, and always more to be done if there's time. Our venture into newspapering was precipitated in a way by the rumor that the then owner, the *Towanda Daily Review*, was going to stop it or make it a page in the *Daily*. So, the Shoemakers (Doc and Stevie) boned up on the possibility of buying the newspaper by consulting text books, talking with Penn State, and examining similar publications, namely the *Hungry Horse News* of Hungry Horse, Montana. The outstanding feature of the *Hungry Horse News* was its use of photographs, and we decided this would be a feature of *The Sullivan Review*. After 40 years, we still use many photos of local events and subjects, with one large photo dominating the front page. We had good mentors helping us to continue the paper; among them were Dave Turner, the owner/publisher of the *Towanda Daily Review*; Ash Parsons, then the mechanical superintendent who selected the type face for the mast head (it was wooden block type); and Carl "Pudge" Raub, who taught us how to make up a page. Others who helped were Marcia Field, our original electronic typesetter; Carl Carlson and Carl Manley, who ran the then commonly used Linotype (hot lead typesetters); in Dushore we had the good advice of Helen Murphy, the *Daily Review*'s clerk in the Dushore office. Also helping the new owners in Dushore were Marge Sheleman in the office, Joyce Dudash and Betty Reibson in advertising, Sally Millard (later Dieffenbach) in photography, and Dottie Masteller. Somehow, with the help of our kids and the McMahon kids we got a paper out each week. When we first took over, the paper was published on Friday, but we soon realized a Friday print date wasn't the best for advertisers. So we changed the publishing date to Thursdays. Papers went in the mail on Thursday morning, leaving Dushore around 7:15 a.m. [Publication as of 2014 is on Wednesdays.] Postal regulations and changes were always a challenge. At first, we single-wrapped each paper. Later, we could bundle. The latest twist is no more mailbags (up until summer 2006, it was about 100 bags per week). Now the papers are placed in tubs, each address label with a bar code, so that sorting is by optical scanners. Circulation in 1966 was about 2100 copies per week, and all the mailing went into six (6) mail bags. Now the 7000 (plus or minus) copies fit into a vanload of mail tubs. Prior to 1969, the office and mailroom were housed in an old building, now gone, that was on the site of the Dushore Market. The paper would be printed Wednesday night around 10 p.m. and then hauled to Dushore. Early Thursday morning (like 5:30 a.m.) the family would address and mail the papers in Dushore and then go to Frank's Lunch for breakfast. Frank Bernatavitz ran a Main Street lunchroom that is now Pam's Restaurant. Sometime in 1969 we moved the mailing operation to the railroad station, which served that purpose until 1979, when it moved to the Sullivan Review Print Shop. Assisting in mailing and circulation over the years were Mildred Marshall and Mary Hokkanen, and now Rose Gumble. Of course, everything in typesetting, photo reproduction and circulation is now on a computer. The newspaper industry continues to evolve with new procedures springing up all the time. Who knows where we'll be going in the future? *The Sullivan Review*, August 31, 2006, p. 1.

## Pudgie, My Teacher

As we signed the documents that gave the Shoemakers ownership of *The Sullivan Review* 18 years ago, Dave Turner, Sr., then publisher of the *Towanda Review*, and also president of the Towanda Printing Company, said to me, "Now, Doc, you'll need Pudgie. I'll make arrangements for him to help you." Until that time I had known Pudgie [Carl "Pudge" Raub] to see him, that's about all. He was easily recognizable by his stature and his frequent trips through town in a specially equipped automobile. Pudgie was an expert compositor, or, more simply, an expert at assembling pages of an offset newspaper, such as The Sully. It was Pudgie who taught me and other members of the staff the fine art of putting more news on a page than anyone would think possible. If it didn't fit, he'd make it fit - with scissors he'd nip off a line or two or spread a line outward. I can still hear him saying, "More news, more news, let's get this thing together today." Funny, when I repeat those lines, I get in trouble. No one got mad at Pudgie. He could turn off an angry cop in New York or wherever, and he could turn on a carload of girls to chauffer him about. Pudgie was a great collector of hats. One in particular was a New York City police officer's cap with a "Canine Corps" patch on the front. When an officer questioned him about it, with the remark that since he was no larger than a big German shepherd, how could he be an officer of a canine unit, Pudgie had a ready answer: "I'm in charge of Chihuahuas." Another story related by his friend Leonard Shultz of Towanda, who operated one of Pudgie's favorite bistros, was the time Pudge showed up at a party, after it was well underway, wearing a Greek fisherman's hat and a dark blue blazer. He rang the doorbell, pounded on the door, and when no one seemed interested to answer he threw open the door and shouted, "Who ordered the taxi?" On Halloween, Pudge had the perfect costume. He'd come as he was. When reminded that he was supposed to be in costume, he'd reply, "I am. I'm here as a midget." *The Sullivan Review*, September 13, 1984, p. 3.

## Sullivan County's Early Newspapers

It's really not news that in today's computer necessary world people are into electronic social networks such as Face Book and YouTube, sending blogs and tweets to whomever will read them. Go back 150 years, more or less, to the 1850s when a lot of people had printer's ink in their veins; their outlet was to print a weekly newspaper. There was no newspaper prior to 1850 in Sullivan County, but in 1850 the *Sullivan Eagle* was started in Dushore by Isaiah Barclay and A.J. Dietrick. When Laporte became the county seat it was moved there. About the same time Michael Meylert started the highly political *Sullivan Democrat* and actively campaigned against Abraham Lincoln. Of course, Lincoln won. Not to be outdone by a Democratic newspaper, in 1865 T.J. Ingham and J.T. Brewster published the (Republican) *Free Press*, which moved to Dushore in 1869 under the editorship of Mr. Brewster. Meanwhile, Ingham started another newspaper in 1872, the *Grant Standard*, supporting U.S. Grant for president. After the election the *Free Press* and *Grant Standard* were merged as the *Press and Standard* and published in Laporte at least through 1876. The Democratic publishers did not give up easily; in 1870 two Democratic papers that didn't last very long appeared, the *Laporte Journal* and the *Dushore Journal*. In 1864, the *Day Star of Zion* and *Banner of Life* appeared as a monthly piece published by Peter Armstrong, the man who deeded his Laporte property, the place now known as Celestia, to God. It may have continued for several years, but died when the religious colony departed the area. In February 1878 the *Dushore Review* was started by Alfred B. Bowman as a weekly tabloid sized newspaper, but after a few months, it was enlarged to broadsheet and the name changed to *The Sullivan Review*. It remains politically independent today, presenting local, county and community news without getting involved in a lot of controversy or gossip. *The Sullivan Review* over the years has had several owner/editors, among them William S. Holmes, A.E. Strong, Fred Newell (1885-1906), Leroy Taylor, Rev. W.K. Shultz, H.M. Wilcox and B.T. Martin (1916-1959). In 1959, B.T. Martin sold it to David Turner of the Towanda Printing Company, who published it with Demarest Berry as editor. In 1966, when Towanda was about to incorporate *The Sullivan Review* into the *Daily Review*, it sold the paper to the Shoemakers, who continue to publish it. Over the years, between the 1880s and early 1900s, other weekly papers were published for some time, then merged with each other or closed altogether. In 1883 and 1884, the *Sullivan Republican* was published by Sam Colt and William Cheney, changed to the *Republican News Item* in 1896 and edited by Charles Wing in Laporte until 1922. It then merged with *The Sullivan Review*. From 1887 until 1921, George Streby edited and published the *Sullivan Gazette*, a Democratic political weekly. Eventually, the *Gazette* was merged with the *Sullivan Herald* (John Scouten and Victor Hugo, editors) to become the *Sullivan Gazette and Herald*. This merger continued until Mr. Streby died in 1921. A successor to the *Gazette* and *Herald* was the *Shunk Star*, which lasted only a few weeks. Much of this information was taken from Streby's *History of Sullivan County*

(1902) and from Myrtle Margargel's section about local newspapers in the booklet "Historical Hodge-Podge." Many pages of remaining copies of old Sullivan County newspapers have been microfilmed.

*The Sullivan Review*, September 2, 2009, p. 13.

## The *Sullivan Gazette* for 1898

Lois Norton and her son, Marlin, stopped by The Sully office earlier this week with an old copy of the *Sullivan Gazette* dated September 8, 1898. What differences in the last 108 years. One of the first things noticed: most of the names mentioned are no longer here–Mingos, Cook, Cavanaugh, Curran, Donahue, Biddle, Deegan, Leverton, Hoffa, Osler, Hermann, and Reeser, to name a few. If you wanted to go to Niagara Falls, you could do so from Dushore at a cost of $3.75 on the Lehigh Valley train. The Laceyville Band Fair was held; the Bernice Band took the $10 third prize, Stevensville Band was first ($40), Wyalusing Band second ($25). Lightning caused two barn fires: barns owned by Patrick Burns near Elwell and William Hewitt on Hatch Hill burned to the ground, nothing saved. Dr. H.N. Osler, the dentist on Main St. next to Dr. Hermann's, advertised extractions for 25 cents, all work guaranteed. Guy Baker of Dushore advertised a pair of three-year old colts–cheap! George Streby placed a public notice that he was making arrangements to build a building and was in need of money; he asked that all accounts due be paid at once–or else. Lutheran Church services in both English and German were announced by the pastor, Jno. W. Klingler; the United Evangelical Church conducted Christian Endeavor at 6:30 p.m. Sunday, according to Pastor D.L. Kepner. Obituary notices were mostly limited to three or four lines: Thomas Curran of Waverly died Thursday at the age of 100 years. He had come from Ireland in 1840. A. Logan Grim of Laporte died Saturday at age 70 of (apparently) Bright's Disease; the well known attorney and Democratic county chairman left a wife, one son and three daughters. Deegan's Store advertised the latest edition of the *Wilkes-Barre Times*–"the afternoon edition arrives on the evening train at 6:30 p.m."–later news than any other daily. It was noted that A.D. Hoag of Dushore purchased the Forksville grist mill for $3,500, and had it fitted up with the latest new machinery. What will the county be like in the next 100 years?

*The Sullivan Review*, April 6, 2006, p. 1.

## History of the Sully Under the Shoemakers

It's that time of year again–the 22nd annual edition of *The Sullivan Review Tourist Guide* is out. Eighty pages, 30,000 copies. It is inserted this week in all copies of *The Sullivan Review*, the *Canton Independent-Sentinel* and the *Luminary* in Muncy, PA. Additional copies will be available throughout the summer to advertisers and other interested persons. The Tourist Guide has been a popular supplement to *The Sullivan Review* since its first appearance in 1967, when it was 32 pages; advertising space was sold on the basis of "If we get enough advertising, we'll print it." From then on it grew from 32 to 48 to 72 pages, and this year to 80 pages. The "Guide" format, but not the distribution, has also been copied by other newspapers in the northeast. Extra copies are always printed for the advertisers, and a supply is always available at the two state parks, Worlds End and Ricketts Glen. In writing this "Satterfield Flyer," I'm recalling some of those who have helped on the project in past years. Among them–and I say "among" because I may not remember everyone, and certainly not in any order–were Kay Homer, Shirley Boatman, Merri Montgomery, Rick Hileman, Ginny Brauer, Sally Sick Kahler, Betty Reibson, Mary Jo Wanagitis, Leighton Scott, and Connie Hileman Taylor. This year's "Guide" was organized and produced by Carmela Walosin, Kathy Bohensky, Dr. Shoemaker, John Shoemaker, Tom McMahon, Stevie Shoemaker, Chris Shoemaker, Mary Eleanor McMahon, Rose Gumble and Bob McGuire, plus all those students in Sullivan County schools who contributed essays. The "Guide" was printed this year by Grit Printing Co. of Williamsport.
*The Sullivan Review Tourist Guide*, May 19, 1988, p. 4.


## Drive West Through Wooster, Ohio, December 1976

The editor, taking a cross country drive in a blizzard in 1976 on Interstate 80, made these notes: by the time we crossed over into Ohio things looked better. The western sky had cleared and the evening star shined ahead of us. We made the 360 miles from Dushore in about seven hours, arriving in Wooster, where, it is claimed locally, Christmas trees were introduced to America in 1847 by a young German immigrant named August Imgard. It is also home base for the Micro-photo Division of Bell and Howell, the people who put *The Sullivan Review* on microfilm and maintain the original film copy in their archives. One of the reasons for our stop here was to deliver some old copies for microfilming–the *Sullivan Democrat*, 1852-1864, and the *Gazette and Herald*,

1887-1899. We hope to visit the micro-photo people first thing tomorrow.

*The Sullivan Review*, December 16, 1976. p. 3.

## Hermit of the Kahill Writes Column No. 1000 – "The Satterfield Flyer" Congratulates the Hermit

Sustained by a daily supplement of spirits mixed with mountain spring water or ice, the Hermit of the Kahill has produced his 1000th column for *The Sullivan Review*. His columns have had a lot to do with the success and continued subscriber and reader interest in this newspaper. It was 20 years ago on September 2nd, 1966 that the present publishers began their tenure with The Sully, having purchased the weekly from the Towanda Printing Company. About one week after our first edition rolled off the press, we had a call from a long-time friend who suggested we should have a local interest column. We agreed, he agreed to write it and named the weekly column "Hermit of The Kahill." Living alone in a shack up on the Kahill (on maps, it's Cahill, after a pioneer family name) with only a hound dog for companionship, no lights, no phone, no running water, gave the Hermit plenty of time to think and read old magazines and newspapers that arrived erratically. He's still there, but has acquired a few conveniences, the latest being electricity–real electricity, not the old Delco System. That means he can have a refrigerator and make branch

Winter scene with typical dairy barn, silo and milk house in Cherry Township. February 1, 1990.

water ice cubes for his gin. Incidentally, Herm prefers the gins with "better botanicals." In addition to writing his 1000th column, the Hermit this week notes his 68th birthday and to celebrate may even get to town for an ice cream cone. We should note that several years ago we published a collection of Hermit columns in a book called *Musings On The Mountain*, which included photographs of local interest taken by *The Sullivan Review* photographer. The book is no longer in print and all copies have been sold. If you have one, it's a collector's item. It doesn't seem possible that we have been newspapering for 20 years or that Herm has been sending a column for that period; his column has travelled by mail and by courier all over the world, to every continent; it has been read in Moscow, London, Tokyo, Guayaquil, Honolulu, Fairbanks, Bombay and Helsinki. We want to take this opportunity to thank the Hermit, express our appreciation for his great contribution to *The Sullivan Review*, and to wish him many happy returns on his birthday. *The Sullivan Review*, August 14, 1986, p. 1

## It's Time for the "Guess How Much Snow Contest"

It's that time of year again, the time the winter watchers have eagerly anticipated–it's time for The Sully's annual "Guess How Much Snow Contest," a game proposed by Sullivan County High School math teacher Don Chubbuck in 1979. *The Sullivan Review* sponsors an annual contest for all would-be meteorologists to guess how much snow will accumulate in the county during the five-month period October to April. Guessers are allowed to use whatever prediction methods they wish–farmer's almanac, crystal ball, woolly bear caterpillars–to make their guess. The only rules: the guess must be on an official entry form and mailed (or delivered in person) to *The Sullivan Review* office in Dushore by noon on December 1, 2013. Snowfall amounts are measured by the Sullivan County Emergency Services office at Laporte and will be measured monthly from now until April 30, 2014. Participants will guess how much snow will fall during that time period. Contestants may make predictions as finite as the nearest 1/100th of an inch (0.01") if they wish. The grand prizewinner, or the guess that comes closest to the actual amount of snowfall WITHOUT going over, will receive $2 per inch; second place will receive $1.50 per inch and third place will win $1 per inch.

*The Sullivan Review*, October 16, 2013, p. 1.

fig. 5

Pauline Holcombe's holding barn
on Little Loyalsock Creek, Dushore.
February 20, 1975.

Santa and young friend. December 24, 1980.

## Travelling With Santa Claus

In order to help Santa Claus get all his work done this time of year and see that he gets to every nook and cranny of Sullivan County, *The Sullivan Review* has for several years sponsored a visit by the "old gent" to many of the country stores in the county. It's great to go along with Santa, take a few pictures and see the expressions on little faces as they tell him their Christmas wishes. Among the many requests we heard were: "Santa, do you think you could bring my Daddy a new house? This is what he would like!" What can Santa say to that? He'll do his best, depending on the prime rate. Another voice, "If you can bring me something, OK, and if you can't, that's OK, too. But don't forget my sister." Then there were three children from one household who each asked for a real live kitten, Mickey Mouse books and shoes. Well, Mom will be busy. Surprising, perhaps, most children asked Santa for things like clothing and shoes, books and items that would have more lasting value. Many of the little girls asked for cosmetics. Santa's favorite note had five little words: "I love you Santa Claus;" he will always love little children. One youngster asked Santa if he ever used swear words. "Never," said Santa. The reply to this was, "Well, my Daddy swears." Of course, the reward for keeping Santa going is that it helps everyone recognize and observe the meaning of Christmas, Christmas for kids, for parents, and grandparents, the wild birds and the pets in the house, friends near and far. Christmas is for paying attention to the lonely and those unable to be up and around, and to remember those no longer with us. Merry Christmas to all and may the New Year be prosperous and abundant.
*The Sullivan Review*, December 24, 1980, p. 2

# Section 2

*Dushore's Beginnings, Postcards*
*from the 1890s on*

# van Revi

Weathered hemlock
free-standing barn, 1973.

## Du Petit Thouars

Sometime before Marie Antoinette was scheduled to arrive at French Azilum in nearby Bradford County, she sent a French Naval Officer to the area to make some necessary arrangements. We assume that Du Petit Thouars did this, and that he later explored the surrounding territory. He eventually built a cabin in a little spring-fed hollow some 20 miles southeast of the French Queen's retreat. He was one of the first non-residents to get his feet wet in the Loyalsock. His name, not easily understood by natives, was shortened and phonetically pronounced "DuShore," later Dushore. The spring-fed hollow became known, later, as Jackson's Hollow. Around April 6, 1852 the postmaster general declared that whatever it had been called, it was now going to be Dushore as far as the post office was concerned. Just recently, a news item received at *The Sullivan Review*, made a reference to a modern French destroyer, *Du Petit Thouars*. Two American naval vessels, the *USS Brown* and the *USS Valdez* visited Brest, France last month for a special 198th anniversary commemoration of the first official recognition of the stars and stripes by a foreign country. Ceremonies during the four-day visit included a wreath laying at a World War I American Naval monument and a reenactment of the historic 1778 visit by John Paul Jones to France. The *USS Brown* exchanged gun salutes with the destroyer *Du Petit Thouars* near the site of the original gun salute between the American ships *Ranger* and *Independence* and the French fleet. In honor of the event, Vice Admiral D'Escadre Le Franc, Commander of the French Atlantic Fleet, was presented a "Don't Tread On Me" Navy Jack by the commanding officer of the *USS Valdez*. City officials of Brest and French Navy officials witnessed the ceremonies from the American ships.
*The Sullivan Review*, April 29, 1976, p. 18.


## A Trip on the Towanda Indian Path

The modern highway system in Pennsylvania includes some 41,000 miles of state roads, but 300 or 400 years ago Indians of Pennsylvania had a network of paths of almost equal mileage. Some 200 of these paths are described and documented in the book *Indian Paths of Pennsylvania* by Paul A.W. Wallace (1998, reprinted from 1965). Indian paths were not only trails through the mountains, but channels of trade and culture for an unknown number of years prior to the coming of the white man and his missionaries. Dr. Wallace described in detail about 200 of these Indian routes, two of which,

the Towanda and Wyalusing Paths, traversed Sullivan County. The Towanda Path ran from Muncy to Towanda on a route nine miles shorter than the present paved highway. The Path, beginning at its southernmost point, originated at Munsee and Shawnee Indian settlements a short distance from the West Branch of the Susquehanna River. It ran northward along the east bank of Wolf Run, following the ridge to Huntersville, then on to Highland Lake. From there the path continued to a location known as Camp Genesee (likely an overnight stopping place), then downhill along Ogdonia Creek to meet the Loyalsock Creek; then it went upstream to Hillsgrove and forded the creek. Just north of Hillsgrove it continued upstream along Elk Creek to Lincoln Falls, then uphill to a ridge leading to Eldredsville and Hugos Corners. Heading north from Hugos Corners, the path went along the southern edge of the Cahill Mountain to Chilson Run, downstream to the Millstone Creek and eventually to Powell. From there the path followed Towanda Creek to its mouth on the Susquehanna River at Towanda. As early as 1799 this path was known as the Genesee Road, a main route for emigrants from southern Pennsylvania to the valley of the Genesee River in New York State. Some historical accounts note that sites along the route were used as encampments. One report noted that as late as 1949 the path was open from Huntersville to Ogdonia. It would be interesting to see how much of the path can still be traversed by automobile, although not a trip for winter or early spring. Maps of portions in Sullivan County and Bradford County, known as No. 10 Highway Maps, could provide guidance over some of the roads.

*The Sullivan Review*, February 20, 2008, p. 5

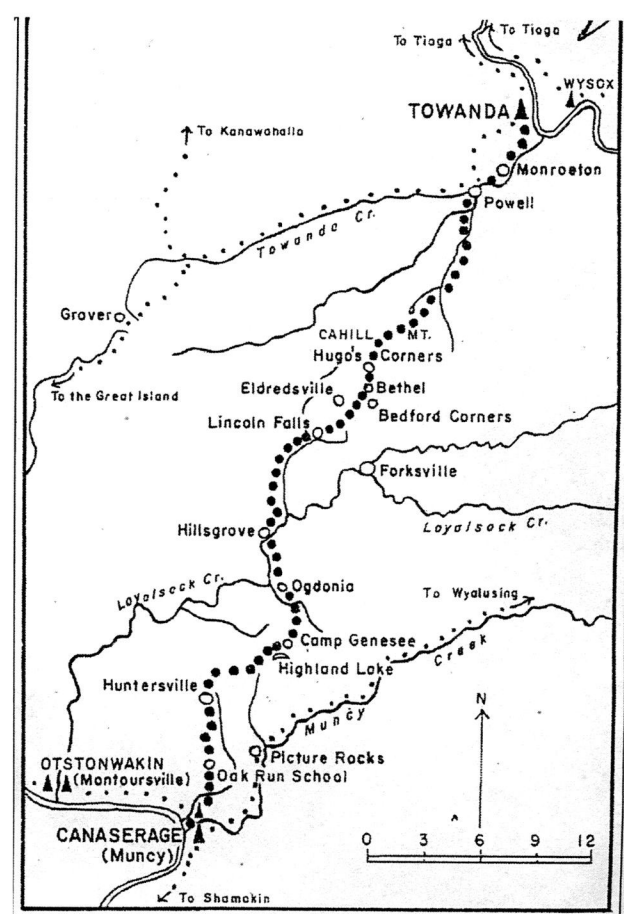

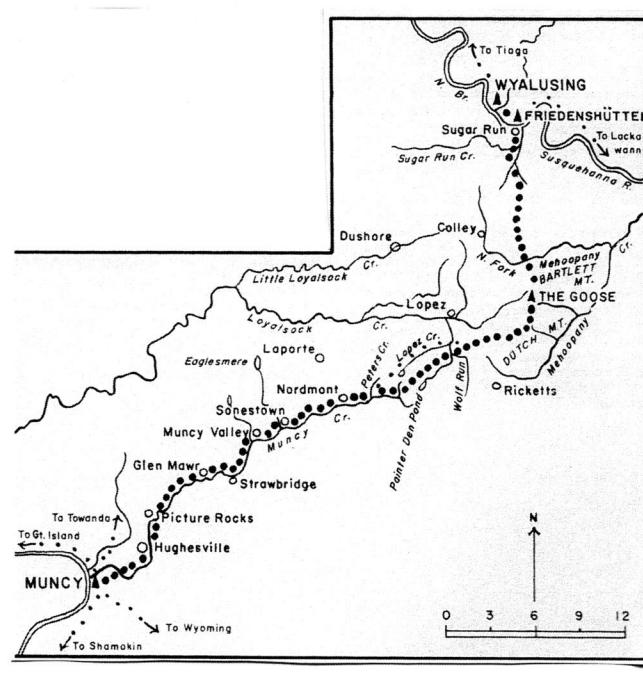

Top: Towanda Path, also known as the Genesee Road.

Bottom: Wyalusing Path.

Maps from Wallace (1965, reprinted 1998).

# Tanbark

When I was much younger, living at home, I remember that the cellar floor was covered with tanbark, a brown powdery substance not unlike sawdust but dustier. It was used as bedding in horse stalls and as a covering in circus rings, among other things. So, where did it come from and how did it become floor-covering material? Many years ago, in northeastern and north central Pennsylvania there were dozens of tanneries producing many kinds of leather, mainly from cattle hides but also from horse and buffalo hides. Why were tanning industries in our part of the state? Because dense forests of lush green hemlock and pine covered the mountains. No one ever thought these plentiful trees could be used up, but now all we see is remnants of this vast evergreen cover. The tanning industry peaked in the mid to late 1800's, when at least five tanneries operated in Sullivan County. Statewide there were hundreds. It all started because hemlock bark contains a good percentage of tannin, the chemical used to tan leather. At the time it was easier to ship hides to the tannery than to ship bark to slaughterhouses. Without tanning, hides don't last long. Centuries ago it was found that by soaking hides in water with certain (then unidentified) natural ingredients, leather could be softened and preserved. The chemical, later identified as tannin, is abundant in hemlock bark. Since most of the hemlock was found in Pennsylvania, tanning became one of six big Pennsylvania industries, aided in no small part by the railroads that hauled hides to the tanneries. In late spring and early summer, bark was easily peeled from huge hemlock trees felled just for the bark, then left to rot. The bark, taken off the tree with a tool called a "spud," was cut into four-foot lengths, hauled to the tannery, ground up and placed in tanks of hot water to leach the tannin.

Top: Ray Reibson, Sr., teamster, hauls bark to a Hillsgrove tannery, ca 1900.

Bottom: Hemlock logs, bark already removed and taken to a tannery.

Well-kept 1884 barn as it appeared in 1972. Small building at
right is the milk house and spring to cool the milk.

Jeff Harriman horse logging in the summer. Horses are much easier on the forest than machinery.

Horse logging in the snow, Harriman and Peterman. January 4, 1996.

The solid material was filtered off and the fluid cooled to continue the tanning process. The spent bark was then dried and used for fuel by the tannery; the excess was called "tanbark," and thus the source of the covering on the cellar floor of my boyhood home. The tanneries in Sullivan County were located in Dushore (don't know where exactly), Laporte (Tannerytown), Muncy Valley (near the present fire hall), Hillsgrove (on the flats, mid town), and at Thorndale (the whole town). There were also tanneries at Tunkhannock, Jenningsville and Noxen. This is but an over view of a rather complicated procedure now done by means other than extraction of tannin from hemlock bark. References used are Tom Taber (1974), *Tanbark, Alcohol, and Lumber,* available at *The Sullivan Review,* and publications from Penn State's Forestry School. Penn State references were provided by Dr. Jim Finley of the Forestry Department.

*The Sullivan Review,* November 28, 2007, p. 20.

## Star Routs (No "e") for Delivering Mail

Spelled without an "e," early mail routes were awarded on a bid basis. Several mail routes were advertised on March 10th, 1864 in the *Dushore Union*, a newspaper published prior to *The Sullivan Review*: No. 2861, from Forks, by Stillwater, Benton, Cole's Creek, Central and Davidson to Laporte, 26 1/2 miles and back, twice a week. No. 2431, from Mehoopany to Furman Hill, Forkston, Lovelton, Bellasylvia, to Dushore, 32 miles and back, once a week. No. 2437, from Towanda to Monroeton, New Albany, Laddsburg and Dushore to Laporte, 30 miles, three times a week. No. 2445, from Shunk, by Eldersville, Campbellville, Colley and Elwell to Sugar Run, 40 miles and back, once a week. No. 2455, from Eaglesmere [sic] by Forksville, Elredsville, and Shunk to Canton, 38 miles and back, once a week. No. 2491, from Muncy, by Hughesville, Picture Rocks, Tivolia ("ia" was used) and Eaglesmere, to Laporte, 25 miles and back, six times a week to Hughesville and three times a week residue. No. 2492, from Muncy, by Wolf Run, Huntersville, Eldredville, Campbellville and Overton to New Albany, 48 miles and back once a week. No. 2493, from Tivolia, by Muncy Bottom and Sonestown to Laporte, 15 miles and back, once a week. No. 2484, from Williamsport, by Warrensville, Loyalsock, Barbour's Mills, Hillsgrove, Millview and Forksville to Dushore, 50 miles and back, once a week. The ad continues: bidders are particularly requested to examine carefully the latter clause of instruction which reads thus: "Under this law, bids that propose to transport the mails with 'celerity certainty and security' have been decided to be the only legal bids, are constructed as providing for the entire mail, however large, and whatever may be the mode of conveyance necessary to insure its 'celerity, certainty and security' and will have the preference over all others, and no others will be considered." So, how come in 1986, it takes five (5) days for a first class letter to come from New Albany to Dushore?

*The Sullivan Review*, July 31, 1986, p. 16 [original title, "The Star Routs"].

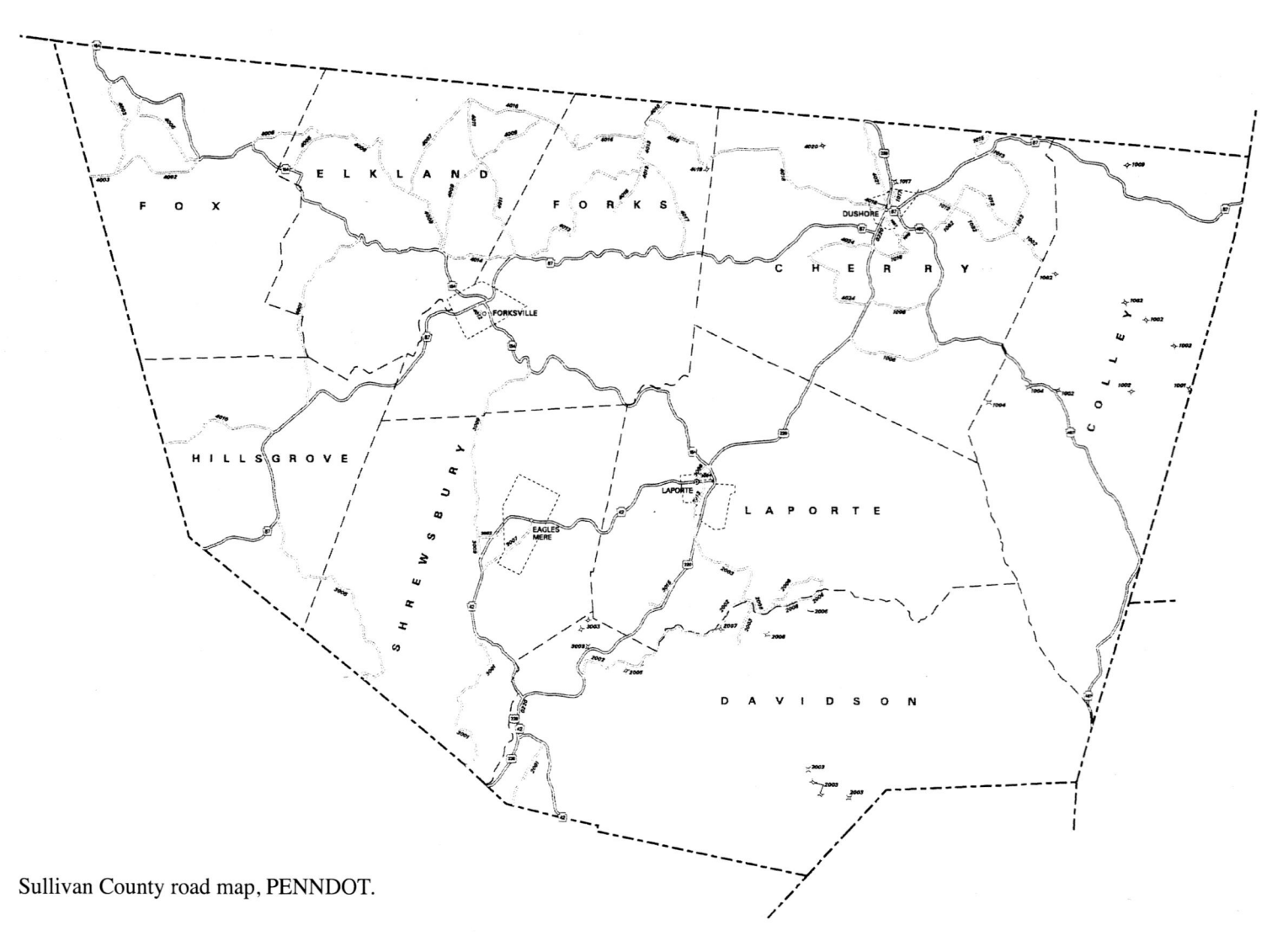

Sullivan County road map, PENNDOT.

## Roads and Road Building

In 1930 Governor Gifford Pinchot's election campaign promised to "get farmers out of the mud." He was elected and soon miles and miles of country dirt roads were paved one lane wide. When I first came to Sullivan County 48 years ago, about four miles of a Pinchot Rural Road, one lane paved with concrete, ran south on Route 87 from Dushore towards Forksville. Concrete for early highway paving couldn't be poured on a hill. The solution was to pave the hills with brick and in the 1920's when Route 220 (then known by another number) came into being in Sullivan County, the stretch coming downhill into Ringdale was paved with brick. Some is still visible around the watering trough. Now concrete can be poured on any slope and carry traffic almost the same day. I recall early concrete paved roads were covered with straw for several days to give newly poured concrete time to "cure." Modern machinery and macadam mixes now cover many of our country roads, replacing gravel, modified gravel, brick and cobblestone. Some narrow roads are being widened. Two lanes in some places are not enough. Urban roads up to six lanes in two directions are often crowded. Progress or just a necessity?
*The Sullivan Review*, December 16, 1999, p. 14.

## Touring and Tooling

Long before cars were powerful enough to spin out or spin tires, travelling a road at a lively clip was known as "tooling along." For what reason, I don't know, except that all cars carried a toolbox on the running board and most drivers could diagnose and repair minor troubles while stopped along the road. Now, as I drive my 500 miles a week through the Endless Mountains, I often think what could be done if my electronically controlled machine would

quit. I'd hope for a nearby telephone. Beyond unlatching the hood, fixing it would be impossible. It would even be a chore to figure out how to jack up the car to change a tire. A report in a recent issue of a bigger newspaper than *The Sullivan Review* mentioned the passing of small auto repair shops, much the same way as mom and pop corner groceries have disappeared. The small shop has given way to the larger ones, those with more modern equipment and enough staff to hold the fort while others attend auto repair schools. It's almost impossible to balance a tire properly without a computer-assisted spinning device that costs a pretty penny. Wheel alignment is another job where sophisticated equipment is needed. And a tune-up–if one is ever needed–requires the likes of a CAT scanner with a graphics monitor. All of this leads to one reason why auto insurance rates continue to rise. And very likely, why more people try to get by without any. And why law enforcement is nebulous or not seen at all. Can the new president-elect do anything about these problems facing the guy who needs a car to get to work, who doesn't live on a public transportation system, and who is a victim of our energy consuming mode of living?
*The Sullivan Review*, November 10, 1988, p. 8.

## Old Postcard from Williamsport

The other day our friend Ed Blossom of the Dushore Car Co. gave us an old hand-colored, German postcard showing a timber raft in the river at Williamsport. The raft was tied along some sort of timbered dock filled with large stones, upon which a group of men were standing and watching rafters prepare for the trip down stream, or perhaps the raft had just arrived from upstream. On the face of the card, written across the skyline, was this message:

"Baer and I walked here from Lewisburg today in six and one-half hours." The card was dated Nov. 30, 1906, and signed, M.E. Haggerty. On the address side of the card was the postmark, showing it was mailed from Williamsport at 5:30 p.m. Nov. 30, 1906. Also on the address side was a second postmark showing the card was received in Lewisburg Dec. 1, 1906, at 6:30 a.m. We wonder if you could do that today–certainly not for a penny postage stamp. In those days trains ran frequent schedules between the two cities and mail was placed on board each train; many times it was sorted en route. Well, we've come a long way, but that kind of service went out with the trains.
*The Sullivan Review*, January 22, 1976, p. 2.

## Postcards for Business Communications Prior to the Telephone

The business world depends on communications. In today's world it's by telephone, computer and fax. Before the telephone, Sullivan County businesses depended on the postcard for everyday communication. Cards came from far and wide by the postal service. A few weeks ago, while sorting over some papers, John Yonkin of Dushore turned up some penny postcards to Messrs Cunningham & Cole, Dushore, proprietors of the local hardware and supply store, where *The Sullivan Review* Print Shop is now locat-

Dushore home with Victorian porches added by the Dushore Construction Co. in the 1880s. 1908.

ed. The simple, plain, one-cent cards were dated June 23, 1890; June 24, 1890; July 2, 1890; and July 9, 1890. Address only was on the stamp side–the postal service would have it no other way. On June 23, Cunningham & Cole received this card from Lopez: Gentlemen: Please ship me via tomorrow's freight one screen door 6'8" X 2'8," your respt. H.T. Lawrence. H.T. Lawrence was one of the Lawrence Brothers who traded as Dushore Construction Co. They built, among other things, the present courthouse in Laporte and several Victorian style homes in and around Dushore. Their style of homes can be easily identified by the acute roof angles and gingerbread decorations in the peaks and fancy spindles.

On June 24, a card came from A.L. Fawcett, jeweler, in New Albany: Gentlemen: If you can't send ice cream dipper tomorrow don't send at all. We want to use it now if at all. Yrs. truly, A. L. Fawcett. Of course, the only regular means of shipment between Dushore and Lopez, or Dushore and New Albany, was by train. At the time, the railroads would take small packages, as opposed to later days when only carload lots were accepted. The Jennings brothers were big lumbermen in the Lopez area and had a company store. All of the cards had a hole punctured somewhere, evidence that Messrs Cunningham & Cole had run the cards on a spike after the order was filled. The last card, dated July 2, 1890, came from Laporte to Messrs Cunningham & Cole from T.J. Keeler, a well-known Laporte carpenter who lived in the house now occupied by the Ray McCarty family, next to Bill Black's Red & White. Mr. Keeler had a big family and it is understood he built a lot of the older homes in Laporte. At the time, there was no train connection between Dushore and Laporte except the daily stage (or mail packet). Keep your eyes peeled for an

old postcard. No telling what kind of story it might tell. *The Sullivan Review*, August 19, 1993, p. 14. [original title: "Old Postcard Tales"]

## Wooden Memories

In this age of sheet metal, fiberglass, plastics, Styrofoam and bubble wrap, it's hard to imagine that many of our common everyday necessities were once made of wood. Following are a few examples of what we used (wooden

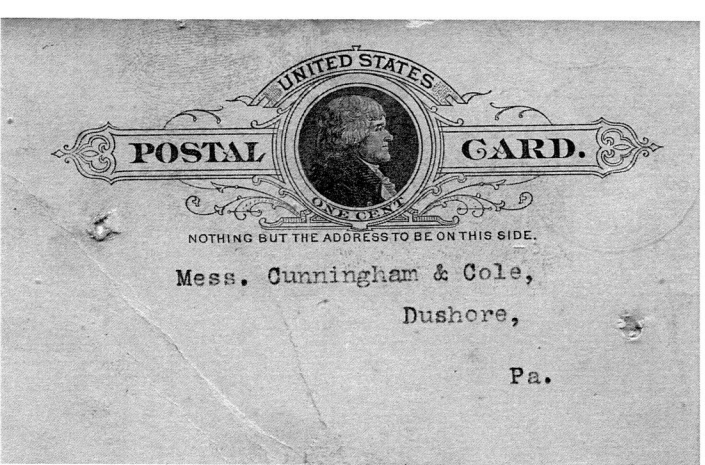

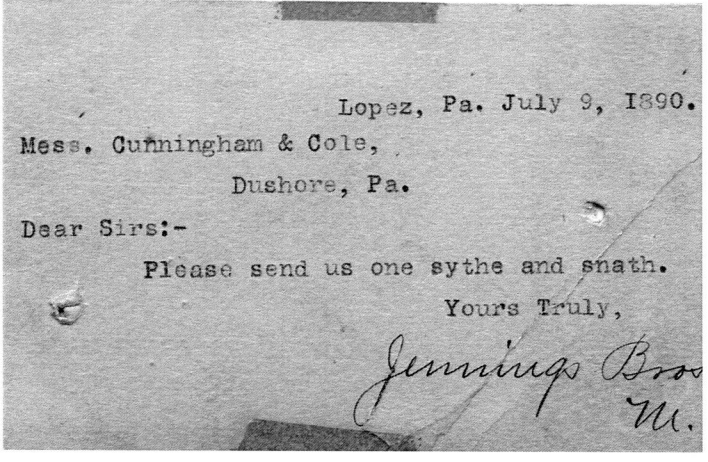

Penny postcards for hardware business orders, July 9, 1890. [A snath is a wooden handle holding a scythe.] Note spindle holes from filing after filling the order. Doc's postcard collection.

ware, if you will), now long gone and hard to find if you wanted one.

Wooden sap buckets hanging on sugar maple trees, collecting sap as it dripped out of the trees through wooden spiles. You might find one in an antique shop. Neatly fitted pine wood strips, assembled to make a bucket, maybe 8-10 quart size, with a hanger to hold it against the tree trunk. The wooden buckets were replaced by galvanized pails with loose lids and metal spiles. Nowadays, a sugar bush is connected by a system of plastic tubing. Goodbye buckets and pails.

When one goes to a grocery store and buys a pound of butter, the butter comes in four neatly wrapped sticks to the pound. It wasn't this way always, because butter was one of the last grocery items delivered in wooden tubs about the size and shape of a bushel basket. The grocer would cut out a chunk, close to a pound, and wrap it in paper for the customer. Refrigeration was not a big factor as most stores were on the cool side, anyway. Some factories made nothing but butter tubs in several shapes and sizes.

When was the last time you saw an automobile with wooden wheel spokes? Early car wheels were fashioned after wagon wheels, wooden spokes connecting the hub to the rim. Wheelwrights were kept busy making spokes for wagon wheels, wheelbarrows, and carriages. Wooden spoked wheels are now hanging lamp fixtures in many business places.

At one time, all freight was shipped in wooden boxes, especially what was shipped by rail. All hardware items shipped to Dad's store were in wooden boxes, nailed shut and opened with a crowbar. The boxes were then knocked apart, the wood used as firewood (I still have one I saved). The merchandise in the boxes was carefully cushioned with wooden wool, commonly known by its nickname, "Excelsior." This finely shredded wood was standard packaging material and is still available commercially. It was made locally in Picture Rocks by the H&E Manufacturing Co. It was especially useful for shipping fragile things, like glassware or china. Now, packaging materials include plastic popcorn, bubble wrap, and Styrofoam. Of course, wooden boxes have been replaced by cardboard boxes of many sizes and thicknesses. Excelsior was a great help in starting a fire in the fireplace.

Of all the wooden memories, wooden pipes should be mentioned. It wasn't too many years ago that Laporte Borough replaced its wooden 4" water main with cast iron. A piece of that pipe may be seen in the Sullivan County Historical Museum in Laporte. Wooden pipe of smaller (inside) diameter was also used to carry water from a spring or well to where it was needed. Pieces are still in the ground at the former Howard Reed Farm in Forks Township. Wood pipe is made by fitting milled strips of wood into a tube of desired size, then strapping it with wire and finally coating it with tar of some sort. Maybe easier said than done. Reports say wooden pipe is still in use in parts of Philadelphia, a testimony of its long life.

The list could go on and on, but all wooden things can be a memory: wooden soda cases, wooden snow shovels, wooden silos, wooden wheelbarrows, wooden fishing boats, wooden auto bodies (Model T station wagon), rain barrels, barrel stave skis, toboggans, cow speculums, snow fencing, cow stanchions, and wagon tongues. Make your own list; you'll be surprised.

*The Sullivan Review*, July 2, 2014, p 20.

Melly Norton of the Sullivan County Historical Society holds a piece of wooden pipe. Pipes such as this one carried water underground to individual households in Laporte.

People lined Main Street for the opening of Route 220 through Dushore in 1928

## "The Big Event Of 1928": The Dushore Monument and Completion of Route 220

On June 3, 2007, I came upon a bit of Dushore and Sullivan County history in a most unusual way. I was attending the June postcard show of the Susquehanna Postcard Club in Danville, PA, going through dozens of old cards at one of the displays. A particular card caught my eye, an image of a huge crowd of people, all wearing hats and gathered around the Monument in Dushore. A speaker on a podium was addressing the crowd, and a band and color guard were in front. August 1928 was the postmark on the card, which carried a one-cent stamp. It was certainly a big event in Dushore to attract such a crowd. Searching The Sully archives we found the reason: "The "Big Event" on June 23, 1928 was the opening of the final section of Route 220 through Sullivan County and Dushore. The day's program included opening the road, unveiling the Monument and two parades. The Dushore Citizens Band left Muncy at 8:30 a.m., arriving in Dushore around noon. The Towanda Band left Towanda at 9:45 a.m., arriving in Dushore at 10:54. The parades met at what is now the red light in Dushore [still the only traffic light in the County], proceeding to the Monument at noon for the ceremony. While the bands played, Mrs. Anna Rush and Mrs. Mary E. Sher unveiled the Monument. Two

political figures addressed the crowd: the Honorable A.C. Fanning (affiliation not noted) and the Honorable Fred A. Godcharles of Milton, then a state senator from Northumberland County. Following this, a firing squad offered a salute and a bugler played taps. The highway had been opened previously, according to the May 30th issue, when then State Secretary of Agriculture C.G. Jordan made it official, but the Monument stone had been delivered to the site just days before the dedication. At some point, the Honorable Frederick W. Magrady, congressman from the 17th District, had obtained some captured German WWI machine guns that were placed around the Monument. A county-wide Farmer's Picnic at Penn's Grove followed the official ceremony, with music by the Naiad-Linta (Firemans) Band of Towanda and the Dushore Citizens Band. Secretary of Agriculture C.G. Jordan and Mr. Frey of Penn State Extension spoke. The picnic continued and the bands played all afternoon; there were all kinds of contests and races for boys and girls. The Berwick Male Quartet then provided professional entertainment, boxing matches began at 7 p.m., dancing at 8:30.

*The Sullivan Review*, June 14, 2007, p. 18.

Dedication of the Dushore Monument, June 23, 1928. Postcard commemorates opening of the final section of Route 220 and dedication of the Dushore Monument, June 23, 1928.
*The Sullivan Review*, June 14, 2008.

## Further Notes About Route 220

Originally, Route 220 was a north-south highway that passed through the county seat of each county it traversed. From the north it passed through Towanda, Laporte, Williamsport, Lock Haven, Bellefonte, Holidaysburg, etc.; it continued south through West Virginia and Virginia and ended at Rockingham, North Carolina. It was a scenic route, built to accommodate cars traveling 30 miles per hour and Sunday drivers. Today's Route 220 does not follow the original, as bypasses have assumed the route designation. Additional information was provided by Rick Mason, communications officer for PennDOT District 3-0 (Montoursville): in 1925, sections of Route 220 were designated as Legislative Routes 17, 16, or 19. It is possible that sometime after 1925, all of the Legislative Route numbers were eliminated in favor of the designation Route 220.

*The Sullivan Review*, June 14, 2007.

## A Tragic Accident, Death in an Old Well

The reported sale of a house on Headley Avenue, Dushore, which has been vacant for over a year, brought to mind a story of the property that happened some 94 years ago. The late Charles Fitzpatrick of the Fitzpatrick and Lambert Ford agency told me of a Dr. William Randall, a country doctor who practiced in Dushore and Sullivan County, who died in an accident related to a dug well on the property. Mr. Fitzpatrick also said the doctor had a very fast horse and could make the trip from Dushore to Forksville in one hour–very fast for a trip of 15 miles, crossing the Loyalsock seven times before reaching the covered bridge. According to information gleaned from *The Sullivan Review* of July 24, 1913, Dr. Randall, one of the best-known physicians in northern Pennsylvania, was overcome by gas in the well and died while trying to rescue Zack Cole. The story of the accident was taken from the newspaper by Betty Ann (Sick) Goodyear, who has a complete collection of obituaries from *The Sullivan Review*. At the time, the water from the water company's reservoir had been unfit for use for some time; Dr. Randall, as well as others in town, decided to establish a supply of his own. An old well at the side of his house was opened and repairs were being made to obtain water. The well was reported to be 90 feet deep, 35 feet of it being dug, the rest drilled. On the Saturday before the accident, a blast of dynamite was used in the bottom of the well to open a seam for water. The following Thursday around 5:30 in the afternoon, Zack Cole went down to the bottom of the dug part to make pipe connections. Cole completed his work and was ready to ascend when he became dizzy and collapsed. Seeing the problem, Dr. Randall went into the well on a rope to rescue him. The doctor had tied a rope around Cole's body and by the aid of half a dozen women who sat on the legs of a tripod to keep them from slipping, Jerome O'Neil and two other men pulled the doctor and Cole up to about 10 feet to the top of the well. At this point, Dr. Randall called up and said he felt faint and wanted to rest. The telephone service had just arrived to town, and Harland McCarty, a clerk in Pealer's Drug Store, came to help. McCarty descended into

the well, but before he could get a rope around Dr. Randall's body, the doctor slipped, or became unconscious and fell to the bottom of the well. Cole was then pulled out, as was McCarty, who fell to the ground unconscious. He was soon revived but Cole remained unconscious for two hours and was in critical condition the next day. As soon as McCarty and Cole were out of the well, Robert Pealer was lowered to the bottom where he found Dr. Randall in a crouched position with his head underwater. Pealer could not get the rope around Randall's body, so he locked his arms around Randall and both were pulled from the well. Pealer was nearly overcome, as well. Dr. Randall's body was taken to the porch, where six doctors worked four hours to revive him before giving up. The exact cause of death was unknown, but it was not due to drowning, as there was no water in his lungs. The doctor's head and body were badly bruised and it was reported he had fractured his skull from the fall. Dr. Randall, at the time, was 46 years old and was married to the former Della J. Fleming of Forksville. They had no children.

*The Sullivan Review*. March 1, 2007, p. 16.

Shocked corn, C. Durwood Ferrell farm, Sonestown, 1977.

Anna Borick with the last family cow in Lopez, 1967. Lopez
was largely populated by eastern European and Russian people
who belonged to St. Vladimir's Russian Orthodox Church or
SS. Peter and Paul Byzantine Catholic Church. Anna dressed
in a native apron, blouse and headband. Residents of the town
worked in logging, mining, and railroad activities.

## From Mud Roads to Super Highways– Advances in Rural Roads

After viewing scenes from the countryside in Afghanistan, I thought of some of the changes we've seen in this country over the last 80 years. I wonder what the USA would look like if we, as a country, had not had the progress and things we take for granted now. We've gone from one-lane dirt roads to Pinchot Rural Roads to two-lane and four-lane divided highways. Who remembers the one-lane road from Dushore to Cherry Mills? We've gone from using horses as farm power to steel wheel tractors to rubber-tired four-wheel drive monsters. Did you know they once said rubber tires would never work on a tractor? You have to be 65 years or older to remember the steam locomotive coming through Dushore. Four trains and a gasoline powered single car stopped each day at Dushore. Some of our commonest water conveniences have changed: indoor running water, indoor facilities, shower baths. Did you ever take a bath in a wooden tub? Our first radios had 200-foot outdoor aerials to pick up signals for the vacuum tube radios. Now, no aerials, no vacuum tubes. Party line telephones gave way to private lines and wireless instruments. Can you remember hand-cranked phones in Dushore and Estella? We've gone from homemade 32-volt electricity (Delco Systems) to rural electric service. No more acetylene gas tanks buried in the back yard. The first time I drank pasteurized milk was in college at Penn State. Before then, raw milk was delivered to houses by a local farmer using a six-quart tin pail that had been cooled overnight in a spring. And speaking of cooling, do you know what an icebox is? The A&P Markets and American Stores had a hard time competing with mom's home-canned fruits, vegetables and meats. There was no frozen food. If you were a kid and got a chest cold, the standard at-home treatment was a mustard plaster or a flaxseed poultice. They've given way to antibiotics and decongestants, which may or may not work better. In the days of manual farm labor, corn was cut with a corn cutter, one stalk at a time. The stalks were then gathered and shocked. Today, we have six-row corn harvesters, no shocks for rabbits or ring-necks. Other farming memories recall flailing beans on the wagon house floor. Do you know what a flail is? And the family cow has disappeared, replaced gradually from a 10 or 15-cow herd to herds of 100 or more. The last family cows in Sullivan County were at Lopez (Anna Borick) or Mildred (Fillie Buzako). I remember testing them for tuberculosis. Well, this column should provide enough fodder or birch bark to chew on for some time. Enjoy your memories. They are better than TV and don't cost a thing. *The Sullivan Review*, November 1, 2001, p. 4.

## Coming and Going–People in the County, 1890-2011

Where did all the people come from? What did they do? Where did they go?

Over 100 years ago, Sullivan County was a more or less isolated area in north central Pennsylvania, served mainly by a railroad and numerous wagon trails, many dug out of mountainsides. Yet in 1890 the census said 11,620 persons lived in the county; in 1900 the number jumped to 12,134. That prompted the questions at the top of this story. Where from? An influx of immigrants from Eastern Europe, Ireland, and Germany arrived to help build the railroads, do local mining and timber off the forests. What did they do? They cleared and settled on small farms to augment their minimal paychecks. The small farms were mainly subsistence farms, not intended to provide farm products to sell. A few chickens, maybe some ducks, a pig, a cow or two, and a horse or two for motive power. But they lived, raised families, paid for the farm and kept going no matter what. Where did they go? Mostly they went off to find a better livelihood, moving out of the county to cities in the region–Wilkes-Barre, Scranton, Williamsport, Elmira, and Binghamton, then far away places. Some stayed closer to Sullivan County, settling in Towanda, Athens and Sayre, where railroads and silk mills offered opportunities. Looking at census figures in 1890, 11,620 people lived in the county; by 1900 the number increased by 514 persons to 12,134, the only decade during which the population grew. From 1900 to 1910 there was a decrease of 846, from 1910 to 1920, a decrease of 1680. Some of this could be attributed to World War I, when industry needed a lot of workers, plus the draft and the flu epidemic. By 1920 the census count was down to 9520 and 10 years after, in 1930, the population declined to 7499. By 1940, the 20-year decline resulted in a loss of 2016. Again, World War II saw an out-migration likely due to the needs of industries in cities. From 1950 on, the 60 years until 2010, the county's population stabilized around 6000 (see chart). Most of the population losses over the years were noted in the rural or agricultural townships. The mines closed or had limited work. The forests became depleted. The railroads had competition from better highways. The four boroughs in Sullivan County did not have any radical changes in population. The following tables will fill out the story. What do you think the next 10, 20, 30 or 40 years will look like?

*The Sullivan Review*, March 23, 2011, p. 11

Ernie Huffmaster's modern version of a stone-boat, Wilmot Township. Doc drives a sled with wheels instead of the planks or skids used to clear fields in the early days.

| Year | Census |
|------|--------|
| 1890 | 11,620 |
| 1900 | 12,134 |
| 1910 | 11,293 |
| 1920 | 9520 |
| 1930 | 7499 |
| 1940 | 7504 |
| 1950 | 6745 |
| 1960 | 6251 |
| 1970 | 5961 |
| 1980 | 6349 |
| 1990 | 6104 |
| 2000 | 6556 |
| 2010 | 6428 |

Old stone wall marking an old property line in Cherry Township. (Some walls date from the 1850s, the stones collected by hand or with a stone-boat.) April 29, 2004.

| | Year | | | | |
|---------|------|------|------|------|------|
| Census | 1890 | 1900 | 1910 | 2000 | 2010 |
| Sullivan County | 11,620 | 12,134 | 11,293 | 6,556 | 6,428 |
| Cherry Twp. | 2,367 | 2,703 | 2,816 | 1,718 | 1,705 |
| Colley Twp. | 1,662 | 1,926 | 1,998 | 647 | 694 |
| Davidson Twp. | 1,652 | 1,714 | 1,464 | 626 | 573 |
| Dushore Boro | 783 | 884 | 813 | 663 | 608 |
| Eagles Mere Boro | --- | 312 | 184 | 153 | 120 |
| Elkland Twp. | 1,058 | 975 | 847 | 607 | 577 |
| Forks Twp. | 780 | 813 | 633 | 407 | 377 |
| Forksville Boro | 191 | 152 | 109 | 147 | 145 |
| Fox Twp. | 693 | 538 | 659 | 332 | 358 |
| Hillsgrove Twp. | 805 | 686 | 588 | 265 | 287 |
| Laporte Boro | 375 | 442 | 245 | 290 | 316 |
| Laporte Twp. | 443 | 465 | 568 | 373 | 349 |
| Shrewsbury Twp. | 811 | 524 | 399 | 328 | 319 |

# Section
# 3

*Animal Patients and Farm Calls*

Twin Herefords on a farm near Dushore,
half an hour after they were born.
February 11, 1993.

## The Day We Came to Dushore and Tested Cows for Tuberculosis, February 1952

Dirty, melting snow banks lined Route 220. We came in by way of New Albany because Route 87 was closed due to flooding near Mehoopany. At the time we didn't know any back roads, but they were very likely impassable anyway. We came with our little Nash Rambler station wagon jammed full of necessities plus one little boy. The car was odd looking, purchased under a then-incentive plan: buy the car and get $300 worth of gasoline, a very attractive offer to one without a job or any real chance of steady employment. My sister had loaned us enough money to pay the moving van that arrived the next day. We unpacked our things at 122 Headley Avenue (next to our present house), stoked up the hot air furnace and had a tank of LP gas delivered for the kitchen stove. The house was owned by Maxine Lynch, wife of Dr. Walter Lynch of Towanda, who was instrumental in getting us to move to Dushore. At the time, Harrington and Co., the well-known dairy products and ice cream plant in Dushore, needed a veterinarian to do dairy inspections. At an earlier meeting at the plant office on German Street we talked with Abe Snyder, plant manager, Harold Thomas, John Boyle and "Jake" Farrell of the creamery staff, and Bill Gregory, County agent. We were served a dish of freshly made vanilla ice cream. What a treat! Mr. Snyder had some connections with the Commonwealth Telephone Company, and arranged for a private line to our house–Dushore 2-2911–then a rarity, as most phone service was via party lines. We were young and flexible, so we managed. Even though we were complete strangers we found new friends, including the Reese Meehans, Charlie Fitzpatrick of the Ford garage, Les and Rosie Miller in the hardware store, and Attorney Ken Lee, who helped us buy the house next door about a year later. Often we were awakened on a snowy morning by a noisy John Deere tractor driven by Art Rohe, plowing the borough streets. Bob Kast delivered our coal. The day after we moved to town, Dr. Moyer, a federal veterinarian from Orwigsburg, in Schuylkill County, stopped by and gave me an assignment to test cows for tuberculosis in several townships. At the time, the state was trying to eradicate tuberculosis from dairy cows using an intra-dermal test. One drop of tuberulin was injected in the cow's vulva, and after three days the cow was checked for swelling at the site of the injection. If no swelling, the test was negative. If positive, another vet would come to tag, brand and appraise the cow for the indemnity then paid by the state. Few if any cows turned up positive in Sullivan County. The first township I tested was Elkland and my guides and helpers were Kermit Hess and Rit Randall. It took a local resident to know the farms and roads, and that's how I learned to get around the county. Other helpers and guides in other townships were Aloysius "Wishy" Marshall, Harold Fulmer, John McCobin, and several others, names forgotten. Bob Lambert, who joined Charlie Fitzpatrick in the Ford garage, sold me an inexpensive two-door Ford sedan with one of the first automatic transmissions. Joe Lynch, who at the time was in the trucking business and later in his Dushore Dairy, was amazed at how the automatic transmission behaved on a snowy road. The '52 Ford was a good car and lasted for over 100,000 miles. And that's the way things started for us in Dushore.

*The Sullivan Review*, August 12, 2009, p. 13.

Little Loyalsock Creek in winter, January 1981.

## Over Muddy Roads to Treat a Sick Cow at Phil Cain's

The recent television program on PBS Channel 44 featuring segments of Dr. James Herriot's *All Creatures Great and Small* brought to mind one of the first farm calls I made upon arrival in Dushore in the spring of 1952. It was the latter part of March, the snow was gone, but the mud wasn't. Roads then were not improved. Dirt roads were dirt, not modified stone, muddy in spring, dusty in summer, snow covered in winter. Mrs. Philip Cain telephoned at suppertime to ask if the doctor would call at the farm to open a cow's teat. The cow had freshened a day or two before and no milk could be obtained from the right hind quarter. The directions were confusing to a newcomer–take a left, then another left, third farm on the right. Simple enough if you know where to start. Anyway, the farm was reached–at that time there were no familiar landmarks–but not before the narrow-tracked Nash was almost mired three times. Reaching the farm, and fortunately wearing knee high slush boots, coveralls and a heavy jacket, I entered the barn. Immediately to the left of the barn door were the horses, stabled side by side. The harness hung just behind the horses, on the wall, narrowing the passageway to the cow stable. I hoped the horses would keep their hind feet on the ground. Inside the cow stable, which was about 40 feet long, stood 15 cows, so close their bellies rubbed as they stood up in their stanchions. Two small light bulbs, somewhat speckled, lit the three-foot walkway behind the cows. Phil Cain was there, seated on a homemade wooden, three-legged milking stool, waiting for the new doctor. He had placed himself right behind the cow needing attention. He was probably 70 years old, sported a full gray moustache, and was as rugged as any Irishman who lived in Albany Valley. He motioned to the cow, and I soon found that he intended to stay on the stool. He knew the cow, I didn't. I shoved her to one side for enough room to examine the udder and the plugged up teat. The cow, a medium sized Holstein, soon revealed what hurt and I found myself against the wall. Phil was puffing on his pipe, not saying anything. What seemed a "desperately" long time passed, and finally the cow's teat yielded to the knife and the flow of milk was established once again. Then it was Phil's turn to speak; when he found out how much the bill was ($13.00), he fell off the stool. From that time on he was a friend, as was his son, Gerald, who took over the farm in later years. Gerald always recalled that story and both of us had fond memories of the event, although at the time it seemed a disaster.

*The Sullivan Review*, July 26, 1979, p. 13. [original title "An Early Vet Call"]

## Burlap Bag Saves Cow

Up until a few years ago, say 40, most farm commodities such as shelled corn, oats, wheat, dried beans, and potatoes were packaged–read "bagged"–in burlap bags. To refresh your memory, burlap is a coarse, heavy fabric woven from the fibers of jute. Often called Hessian cloth, it was a cheap way to handle bulk farm products and a ubiquitous fixture in most barns. But with the advent of plastic, the trusty burlap gave way and quietly disappeared. You might still find an odd bundle of bags tied up with baler twine in the back of a haymow. Now everything is in plastic bags, same size as burlap and fashioned to hold 100 lbs of grain, cow or turkey feed. Even plastic has given way to extra strong paper. Thinking about burlap, I recalled an incident many years ago when a cow, pasturing in an orchard after a windstorm, was picking up fallen apples, a treat after a diet of dry hay or grain. The cow, a big Hereford, was picking apples when, for some unknown reason, she was startled, raised her head with an apple in her mouth, trying to pop it like a pill. But the apple was too big to swallow and became stuck in her throat, so she couldn't burp and soon became bloated. Her stomach was distended to the point where it was almost a drumhead. That's when the farmer called me, "Hurry Doc! I think she's gonna die." I got to the farm in time to see the cow on the ground in pain. The farmer had a halter on her to control her head. I ran into the barn and got a burlap bag, wrapped the whole bag around my arm (to avoid the cow's molars), pried open the cow's mouth and reached in as far as I could. I grasped the apple, retrieved it as a blast of gas escaped. The cow had immediate relief. As I cleaned up and got ready to leave, the farmer asked, "Do I owe you anything, Doc?" I didn't bother to answer.

*The Sullivan Review*, April 21, 2010, p. 14

## The Cow That Swallowed a Ten-Penny Nail

First, a short anatomy lesson on bovine (cow) "stomachs," so called. Cows don't really have four stomachs, the first three being preparatory organs and storage for the fourth, or real stomach, the abomasum, a glandular secreting organ similar to your stomach. When the cow eats a mouthful of hay or silage, it passes to the front stomach, the rumen, which occupies most of the cow's middle. The cow regurgitates her cud from the rumen, chews on it, swallows it; then it goes to stomach number two, the reticulum. The reticulum is lined with tissue that moves the cud on to the third stomach, the omasum. The lining of the reticulum is often sold at a butcher market as tripe (tasty, if cooked right). The key to this story is the reticulum, the lower portion of which is close to–like an inch away from–the heart. Years ago when cattle spent a lot of time on pasture and grazed along barbed wire fences, they often consumed an odd piece of wire, which was never regurgitated with her cud. Instead, the wire would gravitate to the bottom of the reticulum, set up an inflammation and irritate the heart, which could be diagnosed by stethoscope. Enter Ernie Slocum, a dairy farmer between Dushore and New Albany, with a nice herd of Holsteins. He called me one day to look at a sick cow–not eating, no movement of the intestines and a squeaky sound at the bottom of the reticulum. I made a physical diagnosis that the cow had a piece of metal in the reticulum. The barn was dark, with two rows of stanchioned cows facing each other. Ernie was very thrifty–one 40-watt bulb hung in the darker part of the stable. He didn't need much light to care for his cows. The cows knew him but nobody else. With the cow's head secured straight out, I inserted a 16 inch copper pipe speculum, through which I

Cows in the barnyard eye the visiting vet.
April 1982.

would pass the Muffly Retriever–a strong magnet tied to the end of a standard six foot cow size stomach tube. The tube and magnet were lubricated with a bit of liquid soap for easier passage. The trick was to pass the magnet, so that it would drop right into the reticulum and pick up any iron found there. As this was being done, Mr. Slocum watched with wary eyes–"What's this young vet up to?" went through his mind, I'm sure. As I pulled the tube out, on the end of the magnet was a shiny ten-penny nail, a successful retrieve. Ernie's eyes popped in disbelief. I could hardly believe it myself. *The Sullivan Review*, May 19, 2010, p. 18.

Farmer administers an IV to a big Holstein down with hypoglycemia ("milk fever").
Her hungry calf waits nearby. December 1970.

## The Bicycle Pump

Two old time vets were having lunch at the Jolly Trolley earlier this week, talking about days when small dairy farms were plentiful and veterinarians were called upon to do most of the medical and surgical work on the dairy herds. Dr. Bryan Lee is one of the old timers from Tunkhannock, whose practice for the last 45 years has been with dairy cattle. When he started out there were about 600 dairies of various sizes in Wyoming County. Now he attends about 20 herds. Dr. T.W. Shoemaker, of Dushore, had about 350 dairies in the practice area in 1952; now there are fewer than 20. We concluded that the most interesting time to practice in a farm area was in the years between 1950 and 1970. The small dairies, subsistence type farms, with a variety of animals–pigs, sheep, chickens–provided a practitioner with a full schedule, day and night. As we paid our bill I noticed that cashier Ann Walsh was marking some small cylindrical air pumps used to inflate toys. I asked Dr. Lee if he ever treated a cow down with milk fever with a bicycle pump. He never had, so the following story came up. One cold snowy winter night in the 1950's, the roads in Forks Township were plugged and nothing could get through the drifts. The snow fences didn't help. The plows were stuck, too. I got a call from Eugene Rouse, who had a herd of Holsteins in East Forks Township. He had a cow down, paralyzed with milk fever. If not treated soon, she

Cows in snow at barn near Shunk. January 31, 1985.

would die. At that time his son, Mike, was in high school, and like all high school farm boys, had a basketball court (sort of) on the threshing floor of the barn. I knew Mike had a basketball and must have a bicycle pump to keep the ball inflated. I told his dad to get the pump and boil the needle, insert the cooled needle into the cow's teat orifice and begin pumping. This they did and the increased air pressure within the udder reversed the production of the milk, forcing needed calcium into the blood stream. Basically, milk fever is a depletion of calcium in the cow's system and leads to paralysis and death if not treated. By the next morning, a road to Rouse's had been cleared and I got to the farm to treat the cow with injectible calcium. But there she was, standing in the box stall, chewing her cud. The bicycle pump had done its job.

*The Sullivan Review*, August 4, 2010, p. 16.

# Who Knows? The Nose Knows

One of a veterinarian's diagnostic tools is the nose. Like a smell or not, the nose often gives clues to the problem at hand. Most people can identify or recognize obnoxious smells, with about 5 million smell receptors in an ordinary human nose. But compared to a dog, that's hardly enough receptors to talk about. The dog's smell receptors number about 220 million. That's why they can be trained to identify hundreds of specific odors, from underground gas leaks to illegal drugs, bombs, cadavers, contraband foods, even under water drowning victims. Even if an illegal odor is masked by a fancy perfume, a dog's nose can pick it out. Estimates are that dogs detect odors as much as one (1) part per trillion. In recent research, some dogs have been trained to detect certain cancers on a person's breath–lung cancer with a 97% accuracy, breast cancer with an 88% accuracy. But what about an old veterinarian's ability to detect odors? If the dairy farmer wasn't home when the doctor came, the vet could walk down the aisle in front of the cows and pick out the sick one–the one who wouldn't eat–by the smell of ketone on the breath. Ketone (acetone), a sweet smelling, not unpleasant odor, appears when a cow is affected with Ketosis (acetonemia). An injection of glucose generally solved the problem. After farmers became aware of the odor, they treated the cows themselves with propylene glycol, given as a drench by mouth. A similar condition with the same smell often appeared in ewes, but in these cases, it's a bad sign. Another odor giving a diagnostic clue occurs in dogs with mange. An obnoxious smell emanating from the skin of a severely infected dog is unmistakable, caused by bacterial growth in or on the exudate produced on the skin by mange mites. Many years ago, before the development of newer vaccines, canine distemper virus affected the intestinal tract of a dog; diarrhea with an odor gave a definite diagnosis. Today this is rare because of puppy vaccinations. Dogs are smart with their noses, too. If something doesn't smell right, they pass it up. Our boxer pup, Layla, sniffs every treat offered before she accepts the handout. Other dogs delight in odors, rolling around the ground on something dead. Years ago our old family dog Maggie would go along the shore of the river, find a sucker washed ashore and roll in it before returning home for a certain bath. Now you know why food doesn't taste good when you have a head cold–you can't smell it. So, take care of your nose, it's an important part of your daily life.

*The Sullivan Review*, November 26, 2008, p. 16.

## On Delivering Calves

Tuesday afternoon's rain, a mild shower, not quite warm enough to be termed "spring," reminded me of some farm calls I answered recently in response to cows having difficult parturition, or dystochia, or in common everyday language, "my cow can't have her calf." Why does rain remind me? Rain associated with a falling barometer, meaning bad weather, appears to precipitate the onset of calving, and a percentage of cows always seem to have some kind of trouble. Sometimes the fix is merely straightening out a leg or a little pull. Other times, it becomes a major obstetrical operation requiring positioning the mother, rigging up mechanical helps and calling in neighbors from near and far, even calling the local veterinarian. In one recent instance, it was misting in Sullivan County when the phone rang about 6 a.m. on the day a space shuttle was to zoom off its pad. As the shuttle lifted off, I left home on the call, wondering if it would be an easy calving; I was hungry and wanted a leisurely Sunday morning breakfast, a chance to watch the shuttle. As my little Ford Fiesta hummed across the hill I recalled a maxim of one of my professors: "There's two times when you young fellas will get in trouble–if you're hungry and if you're in a hurry." A vintage Murphy's Law, and I filled the bill. Arriving at the farm after a 25-mile drive, I found a small black and white cow lying on a bed of soggy straw and hay, no sign of the calf's legs or head. Upon examination I found out why, and told myself there was no use hurrying, breakfast was a long time off. The birth canal was small, the calf too big for the available space. The well-fed heifer had directed (not by choice) most of its nourishment to its calf. After two hours, all systems were finally aligned; the calf was born, though not with the explosive force of a rocket launch. After a cup of coffee and an order of toast at Muncy Valley, I felt like continuing my interrupted sleep. Before heading home, I placed a call to the office and was told I had a second calf to deliver. Didn't the cows know what day it was and that it was raining? I reported to the next farm and found the cow "down in the woods," only a short walk. Neighbors carried the gear through the coniferous forest covering one of Sullivan County's side hills. I hung my jacket and shirt on a limb and went to work, secured the tackle to a nearby tree and tried to get things aligned. But this cow had been in labor for some time. The head was wedged, wouldn't move either in or out. The plan was to replace the legs inside the cow, get the head started and then recover the legs, but it doesn't work that easily on a side hill in the rain. Nevertheless, the calf was finally delivered. I packed up my gear and moved on. The third case of confinement in a falling barometer situation occurred a week or so later when I received a call from an excited farmer to "Come and help." I parked my car on the "hard" road and transferred equipment to a four-by-four to go across a swampy meadow, then traveled by shank's mare down a steep hillside to a real swamp along a spring run. No birds were out; heavy mist soaked into everything. There was this poor little cow, down and almost out. A rope finally anchored her head so she could be held in one place. A quantity of lubricant (I wished for a grease gun full of lard) was infused around the calf's body and then gentle, constant traction was applied with a twist–like taking a cork out of a wine bottle, until the bones shifted to a conformation that would permit passage. Out came the calf. The hardest part of the job was walking back up the hill. So it goes. The rain is still coming down and so is the barometer. What was the weather like the day you were born? My mother told me that it thundered the day I came along, no doubt, a falling barometer.

*The Sullivan Review*, April 30, 1981, p. 15.

## Cow on Farm Near Shunk Shot by Bullet

The local veterinarian was called recently to see a cow on the farm of Lamar Battin near Shunk. The cow was not eating and a blood-colored fluid dripped from one nostril. As she was not presently milking, she had been pastured along with some younger animals on an adjoining farm with considerable freedom within a fenced-in area. On close examination, a small round hole was found in the cow's lower right jaw, mid-way between the front teeth and the hinge. The right side of her face was swollen and she could not chew or drink. The left eye of the cow was damaged and severely bruised. She had probably been shot, and salvage was recommended. A post mortem examination found a bullet from a large bore rifle. It had coursed di-agonally from the lower right, up through the bones in and around the nostrils and lodged behind the left eye. Whether the cow had been shot directly or whether a bullet had ricocheted off a stone is a matter of conjecture. However, it should be emphasized that hunters should be concerned with shooting near areas where animals are being pastured, and farmers should pay close attention to animals at pasture this time of year.

*The Sullivan Review*, December 19, 1968, p. 1.

## Beware the Green

Every living creature looks forward to springtime weather. Man and beast want to get away from winter's confine-ment. So not long ago, a pair of sheep on a Wyoming County farm got loose and ran out of the open barn door

Cow with new-year's calf. January 11, 1979.

Cow tends newborn calf.

into the pasture. Almost at once they spotted some greenery, in this case rhododendron bushes along a hedgerow. A word here about rhododendron: the plant is a member of the heath family of latifolial shrubs with leathery leaves. Mountain laurel, also known as *Kalmia*, is a member of the same family, and contains the toxic alkaloid androme-dotoxin. Of course, the runaway sheep were attracted to the plant and savored the leaves. How would they know the leaves were poisonous? In less than a matter of hours symptoms of plant poisoning became apparent: salivation, lacrimation, vomiting, diarrhea, ataxia and weakness. Seeing these signs, the farmer called the vet. The farmer, who was a native of Greece and spoke very broken English, told the vet he had called his mother in Greece and asked what to do. She told him, "Give the sheep olive oil." The symptoms may last several days, but when the vet got to the farm the sheep were getting better. The farmer was told to keep using the olive oil. The vet in this case was my grandson Tom Shoemaker, DVM, who at this writing is with an area veterinary hospital. He was prepared to administer other treatments, such as activated charcoal or IV fluids, but seeing the sheep were improving he decided to stick with the olive oil. In

Twin Herefords on a farm near Dushore. Owner Mary Patusic named the newborn bull Doc, the heifer Stevie. Doc says it's not unusual for another cow to help a mother with multiple offspring. February 11, 1993.

an extensive review of treatment of animals poisoned by plants, the *Merck Veterinary Index and Poisonous Plants of the United States* lists treatments as "symptomatic," meaning "Use whatever works." My old colleague and mentor, the late Dr. Walter Lynch of Towanda, when asked the question of what to use, replied "Whatever you've got in your bag, Shoey," which is about right. There are few, if any, specifics. For some reason our whitetail deer don't seem bothered by mountain laurel or rhododendron. Either they are smart enough to avoid the green or they prefer to browse the ground.

*The Sullivan Review*, April 13, 2011, p. 2.

## A Taste of Mare's Milk

At one time, horses were the main power used to drag logs out of the woods to a place where they could be loaded onto a truck. Few horse loggers remain now; the horse has been replaced by the motorized log skidder, which has several advantages over the horse but also some undesirable things, like doing more damage to a forest's duff than a team of horses would. At the time horses were used they were generally kept at the logging site as long as the job lasted. Onsite boarding was easier than taking them home every night. I recall an October 1965 vet call I got one night from Leo Dieffenbach to come and see a sick horse at his logging camp on North Mountain. Leo had a small sawmill set up and a shed to keep one horse. After negotiating the steep road up the north slope of the mountain, about a mile south of Cherry Grove (above Nordmont), I arrived at the camp at the top of the mountain where the road levels off before heading down grade to Elk Grove. The pitch black autumn night was no help locating the place but Leo was there with a lantern. I looked at the horse; the mare had apparently lost her foal but was not desperately

Horse eyes vet.

sick. She was quiet, not excited. While examining the horse, I checked her udder and stripped a few streams of milk; everything was normal. So I got a clean, empty glass pint medicine bottle from my car and milked about a cup of milk into the bottle. I was also teaching school at the time and the next morning took the sample of mare's milk to my biology class. Several of the students sampled the milk, which has the consistency of what is now sold in stores as 1% low fat milk and tastes a bit salty. Just recently one of the students from the class reminded me of the day she tasted the mare's milk. The student was Darla Anderson Bortz, now one of Sullivan County's commissioners. How did she remember that class after 40 some years?

*The Sullivan Review*, October 29, 2009, p. 18.

## Floating Teeth in Lovelton

When I stopped at the Colley Pub last week to deliver some Tourist Guides, it was so hot and humid that I decided to have an ice-cold soda. Among those at the bar was Frank Ryan, of the New Albany area, former proprietor of the Shady Nook. "When are you going on another trip, Doc," he asked, "like the one you took to Russia? I'd like

Steers come out of barn for a bit of sun on the
Meredith Molyneux farm near Overton. May 1974.

to read about it in the paper." Well, that Russian trip was almost six years ago; I found it hard to believe he hadn't read The Sully since then. "What if I tell you about the trip I took today?" I said. "That's Ok with me. Where did you go?" "Lovelton," a big trip, 12 miles east of Dushore, on Route 87 North, to Wyoming County. I had received a call to hustle out to a farm to float the teeth of an old horse for Alfreda Shotwell. Now, this horse wasn't in critical condition; the enamel points on her molars came about after 15 years or so of munching hay and oats. But these points dig into the inside of cheeks or the outside of the tongue, taking the joy out of fresh grass or newly made hay. I looked in my collection of equipment and resurrected a float, a four-inch rasp attached to the end of an 18-inch handle. I noted that the wooden handle was held in place by a horseshoe nail wedge. One always prefers that a horse is going to stand for this operation, so minimal restraint is used, in the hope that its front feet stay on the ground. Alfreda's horse was quiet; I heard the rasp moving back and forth on the outside of the upper molars, making a nice grinding sound as the points were smoothed off. The float was rinsed off in a pail of cold water to get rid of the filings. I told Frank it helps to be six feet tall when you address a horse; it's not easy to stand on a bale of hay to float the teeth, and besides, you have to be tall enough to hold the tongue aside to make room for the float. Had I stopped at the Lovelton Hotel, I would have talked to Joyce Steele, but she was at the Colley Pub, too, and she was interested in my trip to Lovelton. While the horse was the reason for the trip, I should point out some landmarks seen on the way. Since we're into recycling, I noted that Kemerly Conner's potato storage building is now a pallet factory; that Lew Dieffenbach's John Deere store is now a lumber yard; that W.L. Dyer's dairy farm is now a buffalo ranch,

and the Friendly Tavern is now a private residence. So I recommend a trip to Lovelton. Take time to see the sights, drive to the right, don't short left hand curves, and watch the speed limit. See you on the next horse call.
*The Sullivan Review*, July 12, 1990, p. 15.

## Monday Morning Disease

A recent flurry of items in electronic and printing media, including the *Times-Leader* (Nov. 17, 1992), declare that the most common day and time for heart attacks is Monday morning. So, who really wants to get up and go to work on Monday morning? Very likely the situation is stress related. What prompts this writing is a condition long recognized by veterinarians in workhorses. It is commonly known as

Hereford steers, beef cattle, by broken fence in winter. January/February 1970.

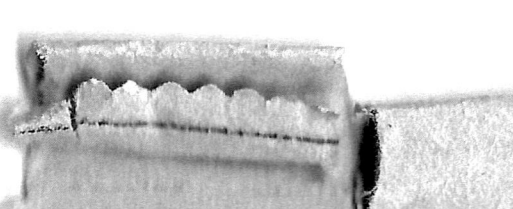

Bill Hunsinger in the barnyard with his Jersey cows, Cherry Township. May 24, 2001.

"Monday Morning Disease," technically Azoturia or Myoglobinuria and various other names (D.H. Udall, 1954, *The Practice of Veterinary Medicine*). The disease is specific to horses, chiefly draft animals; it is characterized by a sudden paralysis of the hind limbs that occurs after a brief period of idleness such as a weekend off with no work and lots of feed. The symptoms, aside from the paralysis, are coffee-colored urine and profuse sweating. Several additional physiological changes may be observed that can lead to a fatal outcome. Predisposing the condition is the weekend off, standing in a stable on full feed with little or no exercise. How many people take the weekend to become couch-bound, consuming inordinate amounts of food and beverages, getting on their feet only during TV commercials? Of course, when the horse was the prime

Cows in brush. It's much harder to treat an
animal in a briar patch. May 9, 1974.

motive power on a farm, a poor farmer with only one workhorse at his disposal had to be cautious of Monday Morning Disease. The coffee-colored urine occurs as the kidneys process degenerating muscle tissue, first the heavy muscles of the hind leg, sometimes those of the heart. The question may be asked, is there some relationship between statistics of Monday morning heart attacks and the stress of getting up and going to work after a weekend off?

*The Sullivan Review*, November 19, 1992, p. 12.

## Pig Stories

Since this year–2007–is the Chinese "Year of the Pig," a few local pig stories might be in order. These were incidents in my large veterinary practice occurring sometime in the late 1950s. The first concerned a pregnant sow that weighed about 300 pounds, lying on her side trying to give birth to her litter of piglets. I was called to the farm outside of Dushore to examine her. The examination revealed that one piglet was unable to pass the birth canal. Unfortunately, my hand was too large to grasp the piglet, so I went home and got Mrs. Shoemaker to try her luck; she couldn't reach the piglet, either, so a Caesarian section was performed. Sows generally have eight to ten piglets, but this one

Piglets running in a field. October 1976.

had only one– the one that was stuck, but still alive. The farmer was disappointed–only one piglet and all that work. Anyway, I returned the next day to check on the sow and guess what? She had eaten her offspring. Responding to another call at a mountain farm located between Hillsgrove and Proctor, I was directed to a dug road up the side of the steep mountain. I found it, but about 500 feet above the main road was a gate and a diversion ditch. I opened the gate, went through, closed the gate and continued up the hill. Came to another gate. Same routine. Finally, the top of the hill opened up to a broad pasture, with huge glacial rocks dotting the field. At the barn the farmer directed me to a box stall where the boar hog was kept. Hogs aren't easily lassoed or restrained, and this fellow kept running around the perimeter of the stall. Finally, the farmer produced a 55-gallon steel drum, open on one end, which was placed against the wall of the stall. In one of the laps round the stall the hog ran head first into the drum. Quickly we upended the drum, the hog's head on the bottom. My assistant, son Jim, grabbed the legs and the operation was over in seconds.

*The Sullivan Review*, March 8, 2007, p. 7. [original title, "Year of the Pig"]

## More Pig Stories

Pigs are intelligent creatures and can be trained. In the late 1970s, the late Ellery Hatch who lived on North Street, the road between Hugo Corners and Camp Brule, had a tame pig. Every afternoon, winter and summer, he would put a halter on his pig and take a walk along the dirt road. Another pig story comes from Albany Township, about five miles north of Dushore. The late Jack Coyle, a big, jolly Irishman, had a part-time farm operation. He usually worked on

Sow and piglets, May 21, 1987.

Two pigs in snow, February 1970.

the railroad in Elmira (or someplace) and his job was to clean out boxcars that had been used to haul grain. Jack swept the cleanings into a bag, I was told, and took them home to feed to his pigs. The farm had an old bank barn, six stanchions along the bank side; the clear side was covered, usually with a high ceiling. But Jack was too busy to haul manure, so the barnyard was the depository. So much so that the "floor" was almost to the ceiling; one had to stoop to get around. Anyway, Jack had a big boar hog–big, maybe 700 pounds–that he wanted neutered. This must have been a Sunday afternoon job, as there was help around the farm. Somehow, I don't know how, Jack got a chain loop around the pig's snout. Pigs don't charge, they back away in such situations. The log chain (maybe 15-20 feet long) was tossed over a handy beam, easily in reach because of the low ceiling. The pig backed away, making the chain tight, and straight away, I stood behind the pig and did the job. Recovery was uneventful. I don't know who got the hundred pound hams.

*The Sullivan Review*, March 15, 2007, p. 11.

[original title, "More on the Chinese 'Year of the Pig']

Two pigs made the front page. *The Sullivan Review*, November 7, 1974, p. 1.

# Section
# 4

*The Veterinary Office*

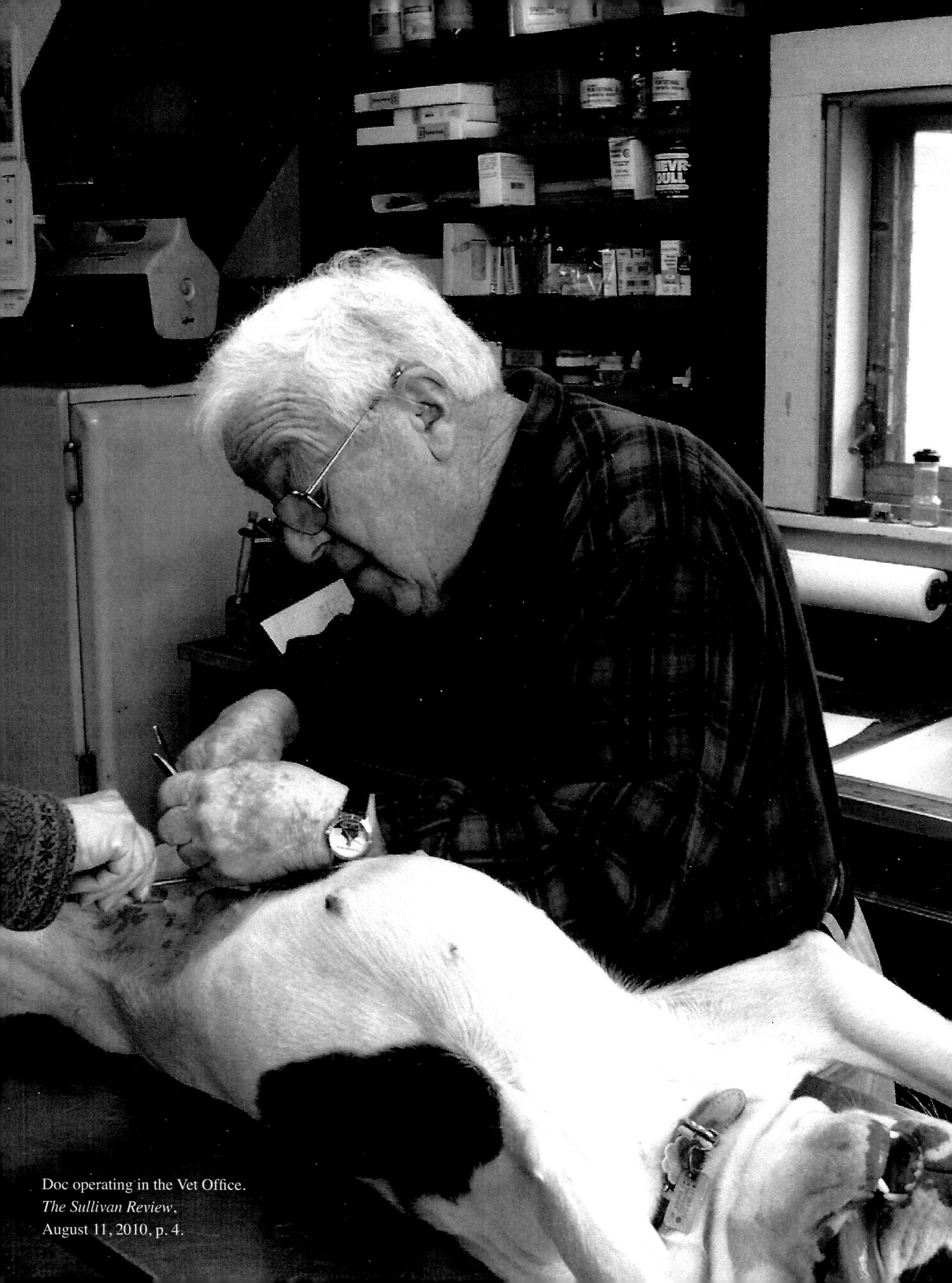

Doc operating in the Vet Office.
*The Sullivan Review*,
August 11, 2010, p. 4.

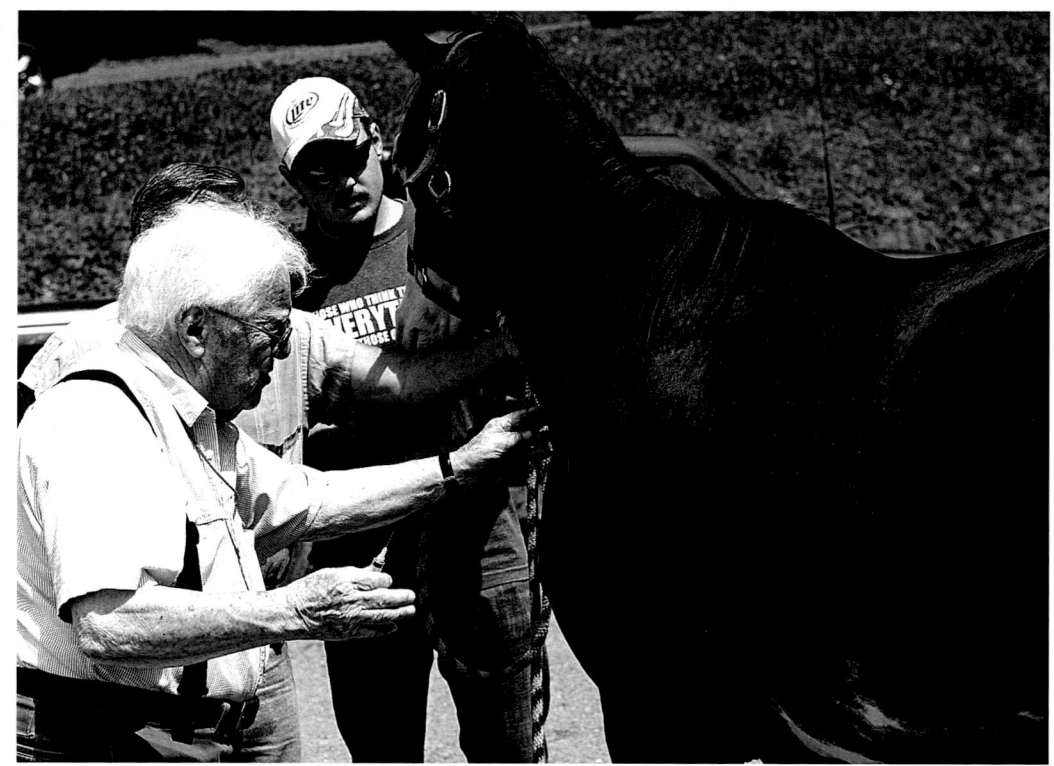

Clinic to blood test competitors at the Sullivan County fair. 2009.
*The Sullivan Review*, August 11, 2010.

## City Dog's Adventures in the Country

We may be getting a taste of summer during our first few days of spring, with gorgeous weather last Tuesday, Wednesday, Thursday and Friday, temperatures in the 60s or above. A busy week was topped off by yet another harbinger of the season–a phone call at 11 p.m. "This you, Doc?" Who else answers the phone beside my bed at this hour? "We have a problem. Our dog just came in with a face full of porcupine quills. We're in New Albany. Can you help us out?  We'll be there in two minutes." "Give me time to get dressed," I said as I rolled over to contemplate the 17th call of the day. While waiting for the two minutes to elapse, I decided to construct the series of events leading to the dog's encounter with the porcupine. A city dog arriving at a cabin after a three-hour drive is all excited about the prospect of a weekend in the country. It jumps out of the car, late at night, and is met by a welcoming committee just taking a stroll about the premises. There's a brief skirmish, followed by a yelp from "City dog" and the discovery by its owner of a snoot full of quills. Two minutes becomes a half hour. The victim turns out to be a 120-pound Labrador retriever, young and active, by now pawing at

its face and slobbering from quills stuck in its tongue. So excited and upset, the dog requires more than the usual amount of sedation; its owner could have used some, too, as he thought of all the dire possibilities of the situation. After calming down, the big Lab stretched out and the quills were removed, one by one. Those that could be seen are no problem. The ones that could be felt and not seen were another matter. There's nothing quite like feeling the dark end of a porcupine quill, the one with barbs, like the barb on a fishhook, easy to penetrate, hard to remove. In dogs that are under anesthesia, the muscles of the lips, face and skin are relaxed, making extraction easier on both beast and man. But now, with the job completed, how do you get this 120 pounder back into the car? Well, you put it in a wheelbarrow and wheel it up to the back of the station wagon. Simple. Even at midnight.

*The Sullivan Review*, March 31, 1988, p. 15.

Another painful encounter with a porcupine.

## Hound Dog "Duke" Survives Unusual Mishap, Almost Drinks Well Dry

While hunting accidents generally happen to humans, some involve dogs. When Francis Richart of Dushore went hunting Saturday, he took his two beagle hounds, Duke and Bullet, as well as his brother-in-law Andy Sweyko of Frackville, cousin Alex Waldron of Dushore and stepfather Melvin Duven. The day was perfect for hunting; the only disappointing factor was a shortage of rabbits. So Francis wasn't surprised to discover Duke missing after a while, because Duke has a mind of his own. If there isn't enough excitement in the field he heads for home. After another half hour of hunting, the party returned home expecting Duke to greet them. But, there was no Duke. Sensing trouble, Francis retraced his steps and discovered Duke going down, possibly for the last time, in an old open dug well on an abandoned farm. He quickly lowered himself as best he could into the well, grabbed a hind leg and got Duke to dry ground. The poor dog was ice cold and not breathing. Fortunately, the veterinarian was in his office and resuscitation was started immediately by using artificial respiration, brisk rubbing with toweling and an injected stimulant. The dog's temperature was 96° Fahrenheit (normal for a dog is 102° Fahrenheit), respiration barely perceptible. The legs were extended and stiff, and could not be flexed. The jaw was set, could not be opened. Besides all this, the dog's body was bloated, expanded from water that he gulped and swallowed each time he went under. Fortunately, not much if any water was detected in the lungs. In his extreme effort to get out of the well by climbing, Duke had worn his front toenails down to the quick. As he began to respond to resuscitation his breathing became regular and his body, while still stiff, began to warm up. He was then placed in a cage with an electric heater focused on his underside. As he warmed up, Duke began to move his legs. A little while later he could hold his head up. Sometime after this, the water he had consumed in trying to drink the well dry was passed and Duke regained his old figure. By suppertime he was able to walk out of the hospital, and the next day he was himself again. A sidelight to the incident was the anxiety felt by the Richart children, who think the world of Duke. Their faces radiated joy and gratitude when they saw Duke walk out of the hospital. One question: If you fell in a well, would you think quickly enough to try to drink it dry? An important postscript to this story is that Mr. Richart filled in the well hole with stones on Sunday to prevent a duplication of the near tragedy, perhaps one involving a child. *The Sullivan Review*, November 16, 1967, p. 1.

## Veterinary Medicine Before Penicillin, Cabinets Full of Remedies

A paragraph or two in the *1942 Yearbook of Agriculture* published by the United States Department of Agriculture caught my eye: "Up to the present time (1942) veterinary authorities know of no chemicals or drugs that when

Doc's house and the vet office, right, on Headley Avenue. November 1969.

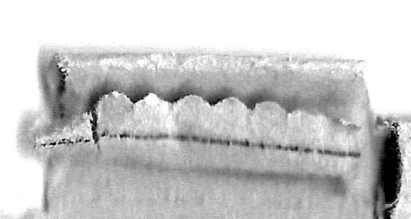

Dr. Daniels' cabinet for veterinary medicines.

Dr. LeGear's Famous Poultry Cures. Many country stores around Sullivan County had cabinets provided by Dr. Daniels, stocked with remedies in powder or liquid form such as physic balls, linament powder, distemper cure, worm killer, gall cure, colic cure, renovated powder, hoof grower and softener, absorbent blister and Kloudy witch hazel. The cabinets were secured with lock and key; the storekeeper would open the door and the farmer would select what he thought he needed. In the case of powders or liquids a small amount was suspended in water and given by drench to the sick horse or cow. In the case of blisters, some would be applied to the sore spot. For a drench, a long-necked whiskey bottle was preferred; in older barns an empty bottle on a barn beam was evidence that some type of medicine had been given. Some vets carried a supply of empty whiskey bottles in the trunk of their sedans along with ready made-up solutions to be administered. Colored solutions were the norm. All this changed after the onset of World War II with the introduction of penicillin, and wider use of

administered internally would destroy causitive agents of infectious or contagious (communicable) diseases of livestock without being toxic to the tissues or organs of the body." Now, nearly 70 years later, we've come a long way in providing many kinds of effective drugs and medicines. But what did livestock owners and veterinarians do before the 1940s? They depended on nostrums, remedies and patent medicines to cure the ailments of livestock. Some common conditions faced by horses and cows include Monday Morning Disease, Heaves, Fistulas, founder, scours, wooden tongue, hollow horn, woof-in-the-tail, choke, Bang's disease, cattle grub, Texas fever, to mention a few. But, wait: there were purveyors of cures for most any situation a farmer might face in his sick or sickly animals. Among them were Dr. Daniels' Veterinary Medicines and

Huskies.

Top: Great Danes, one black, the rest blue merles. Image won first prize in the 2014 *Pennsylvania Magazine* contest for State Symbol, this breed being the official state dog.

Bottom: Yellow Labradors.

sulfa drugs. Sulfanilimide and acriflavine (a World War I antiseptic and wound treatment) had some use prior to the war but they were expensive. The first penicillin available in veterinary medicine in the late 1940s and early 1950s was penicillin suspended in peanut oil, and sold in 10 cubic centimeter vials (about 1/3 of an ounce). For a dairy cow with foot rot, a dose of one cubic centimeter would produce outstanding results. No longer on the market, oil based penicillin has been replaced by water based products. Other early antibiotics were streptomycin, often mixed with milk of magnesia to treat calfhood diarrhea, but no longer available. The introduction of new antibiotics continues all the time. Dr. Daniels' medicine cabinets are now collectors' items,

some going at auction sales upwards of $2,000. Somewhat unaffordable for me, I did find one, measured it and had a cabinetmaker make an exact reproduction after I found a company that made reproductions of the colorful sign on the front of the cabinet. But there are no little boxes of nostrums on the shelves inside the cabinet. Besides, few around now know how to drench a cow.

*The Sullivan Review Tourist Guide*, Fall/Winter 2008, p. 32. [original title: Annals of Veterinary Medicine Before Penicillin]

Wheelbarrow full of German shorthaired pointers.

# Section 5

*Dairy Industry in Sullivan County*

Holstein contemplates what life would be like on the other side of the fence. Dennis and Dave Hottenstein's farm, Forks Township. June 6, 2006.

## Open House at Pardoe Brothers Dairy Farm, Elkland Township

Among American traditions such as house warmings, barn raisings, work bees and quilting parties is the barn warming or open house, one of which will be observed Saturday, November 30th, 1968, from 10 a.m. to 4 p.m. at Pardoe Brothers Dairy Farm near Camp Brule in Elkland Township. The new dairy barn features free stall housing, automated feeding and a milking parlor system that will change conventional ideas about dairying. Modern dairy farming is nothing like raising the family cow of years ago. While 12 cows were enough for your grandfather, today's economic pace demands 3 or 4 times that many for one man. The Pardoes have a barn capacity of 100 cows–large for Sullivan County but small for some sections of the country. The barn was in the planning stage for a long time, until general contractor Henry Epler coordinated the plans and the brothers assisted in doing the work. Materials and supplies were ordered and installed as work progressed. The large silo, a Fickes 24 x 60 concrete stave silo, will hold 760 tons of silage–corn from 50 acres, more or less. Automated PATZ equipment delivers the silage to a centrally located feeding bunk in the barn. The barn itself, made of specially designed Whipple trusses, has only two rows of square poles, but these are treated to last indefinitely. Skylights in the roof provide a soft glow inside the barn, the ridge open to permit plenty of ventilation. The free stall area designed by the Badger Company will have about 12 inches of bedding. The cows can go in and out of these stalls as they wish; they prefer them to bare concrete walkways, which are about four inches thick above a good gravel base. It takes a lot of concrete to cover a barn 76 x 188 feet. Automatic watering buckets are placed at strategic locations, since big

Holsteins can drink up to 35 gallons of water per day. The milking parlor, herringbone in design, is a Universal installation. Six cows will walk in on each side of a sunken work area, from where milkers will be attached and the milk will flow by pipeline to the huge bulk tank. Feed bins are elevated above the milking parlors, and special augers will deliver dairy rations to the cows while they are being milked. Automatic controls regulate milk flow, filtering and later, washing and rinsing of the milk lines. The complexity of the system reminds one of a chemical research laboratory. Bulk tanks vary in design, shape, and capacity; the tank at Pardoe Brothers was supplied by Canton Agway. A feature of the barn is the holding area for five or six cows in conventional stanchions, for use in treating sick animals or examining others for pregnancy and breeding. Electricity, a clean, safe and dependable source of power

Here's looking at you! Ray Norconk's heifers, Wilmot Township. June 19, 1997.

for machinery, plays a major role in the modern dairy. The interior of the loose housing (no stanchions)–feeding area will be lighted with two large outdoor type streetlights. While most of the materials for the barn were purchased, the Pardoes cut down a number of large hemlock trees and had planks sawed at local sawmills for use throughout the barn. Seasoned hemlock has long been known as an ideal wood for barn construction. Behind the entire operation is the hard work of the owners, the assurance of financial backing by one of the area banks, and insurance from a local company to protect the structure. Milk from the farm will be sent to Grover Farms Company at Grover, and will be picked up regularly at the farm by a tanker truck. To see the trend in modern dairy farming first hand, Pardoe Brothers cordially invite interested people to visit their farm on Saturday November 30th, between 10 a.m. and 4 p.m. *The Sullivan Review.*

## Dairy Herd Improvement: Artificial Breeding Methods in Sullivan County

Sullivan County reached a dairying landmark this month with the birth of five dairy calves conceived in December 1981 and transferred as embryos a week later to five surrogate mothers. In the 1920's the Sullivan-Bradford Dairy Herd Improvement Association (DHIA) was organized to enable dairy farmers to improve their herds by selecting the better cows, culling the poor ones and raising bulls from their better cows. Prior to World War II, most dairy farms kept their own bulls. Every barn had a bullpen built to contain a heavy, unpredictable bull that was let out only when a cow had to be bred. Standard equipment in a barn was a bull staff, a long pole with a clasp on the end to grab the bull's nose ring, which generally controlled the bull, but didn't always. Some farmers let their bulls loose with the cows in the barnyard or the pasture. I recall several times making a hasty retreat as a bull began to bellow and paw the ground with his front feet. As time passed, several farmers in the vicinity of Cherry Mills formed a bullring, getting together to buy a good bull and share the services. The bull was kept at the Ambrose Doyle farm by co-owners Frank Rohe and Ralph Rohe. Services of the bull were shared with the herds of Bob Dempsey, Steve Litzelman, Nick Gainer and Ed Gainer. The Sullivan-Bradford Cooperative for artificial breeding of dairy cattle was organized around the beginning of 1945, the first board of directors being Ambrose Doyle, Frank V. Rohe, Harland Baumunk

Three Norconk Farm cows, Wilmot Township. June 13, 2002.

and Lewis Neuber. Ivan E. Waltman of New Albany was secretary-treasurer; others interested in the organization included Ralph Rohe, John Arey and Paul Heiber. The first artificial breeding in the county took place February 2, 1945 by Dr. John Q. Adams, a veterinarian then located in Dushore. Colley resident Bob Pond was the substitute inseminator; he bred his first cow on April 7, 1945, and since March 1, 1946 has been the technician in this area. During his first year, Bob inseminated 580 cows; in 1981 the count was 4000 cows. The Northeastern Pennsylvania breeding cooperative (NEPA), organized on October 20, 1944, began supplying semen from its Tunkhannock headquarters; since then it has been incorporated as N.E.B.A. [Northeastern Breeders Association], and at present does business as Sire Power. While NEPA had representative bulls from several breeds, Holsteins were of most interest here. The first Holstein bull purchased was King Arrow Aggie from the Al Hallock herd in Laceyville and designated H-1. Other proven bulls were Holstein H-2, Piebe Gerben Gremella from the Pete Corcoran farm in Jenningsville; H-5, Penn State Inka Paul from St. Michael's School at Hoban Heights, Wyoming County; H-8, Burke Fobes Abbekerk; and H-16, Lauxmont O'Nobleman from Shoemaker Bros. Sunnyside Farm, West Wyoming, in Luzerne County. I recall when my Shoemaker uncles of Sunnyside Farm went to Canada or northern New York State and purchased O'Nobleman as a week old calf for the then very high price of $350. They borrowed my father's 1936 Ford pickup truck to make the trip. O'Nobleman was raised on the farm and through several years of DHIA testing was designated a "proven bull," as were all bulls purchased by NEPA. Nobleman remained on the line at NEPA for 18 years; some of his offspring may still be around Sullivan County. Technology has advanced over the years from using egg-yoke diluted semen to frozen semen in single service straws to actual transfer of viable embryos from one cow to another. The new technology would make the H-1 class bulls turn over in their graves.

*The Sullivan Review*, September 23, 1982, p. 8. [original title, Annals of Dairy Herd Improvement and the Development of Artificial Breeding Methods in Sullivan County]

Top: Holstein cows in stanchions, 1969. Today most cows are kept in free stalls.

Bottom: Holstein heifers in pasture. 1969.

# Limericks

In a recent column, the Hermit of the Kahill invited readers to submit some limericks and have a contest. Well, we haven't set any rules–except the rules of what makes up a limerick. As for prizes, it might just be your limerick in print in The Sully. If you don't know, a limerick is a humorous five-line piece of verse; lines one, two and five in rhyme, and lines three and four in rhyme. A classic example:

There once was a man from Nantucket

Who kept all his cash in a bucket

But his daughter named Nan

Ran away with a man

And as for the bucket, Nantucket.

The limerick was popularized by Edmund Lear in his *Book of Nonsense* (1864), but at that time the verses were not known as, or called, limericks. One story is that the name dates from World War I when soldiers returning from the European battlefields to County Limerick, Ireland, chanted the verses as they marched home. The subject of many limericks is ribald, raunchy or off taste–not what we want for publication in The Sully. In so-called "modern" limericks, the rules of Lear's verse have been somewhat changed, so the last line ends with a word that rhymes and not a repetition of the last word of the first line. Following the announcement in The Hermit's column we received this from Harry Engle of Camp Hill, PA:

There once was an old Senegalese

Who grew both peanuts and teas

When he found nuts for lunch

Were too hard to crunch

He settled for tea with soft cheese.

Now, that's a good one for June Dairy Month. Thanks, Harry.

*The Sullivan Review*, June 4, 1987, p. 3

Dairy Month triplets, June 12, 1975

## The Holstein Cow Affair, from Sullivan County to Turlock, California

As reported in last week's "Satterfield Flyer," our far west reporter stationed at Palo Alto, California was having trouble finding out what happened to a Sullivan County Holstein cow consigned to the All-Elevation Sale at Turlock, CA. Well, this week we received photographs of the cow and her dam from Merlin Carlson, sales manager of Turlock, CA, and a page from the sale catalog that included a run down of the pedigree of Cherry Acres Patches Elevation, principal in the Sullivan County Holstein Cow Affair. We found she was born October 20, 1974 on the farm of Ron and Tish Hembury of Dushore and sold at two months of age for $1500 to Chuck Will of Willea Holsteins, Underwood, Minnesota. She was raised on this farm and sold as a two year old, bred heifer to the Patches Syndicate of Alberta, Utah, for $5100. The Patches Syndicate established three records for Cherry Acres Patches Elevation. On her first lactation, being just over two years old, she produced 20,307 pounds of milk testing 2.7% (somewhat below what might be expected) or 550 pounds of butterfat. She produced 19,740 pounds of milk, 505 pounds of butterfat on her second lactation, 20,070 pounds of milk, 480 pounds of butterfat (that's 2.4%) on her third. She received a score of 88, "very good" for her class of dairy cow. Cherry Acres Patches Elevation gained interest among Holstein breeders mainly because of her mother, Cherry Acres Queenpin, who had a type score of 92 out of a possible 98, was classified 2-E at seven years, 3-E at nine years and 4-E at 12 years of age. She had a national rank cow index of 1628, placing her in the top 2% of Holstein cows in the nation. Her top production came at 8 years of age when she produced 33,391 pounds of milk and 179 pounds of butterfat,

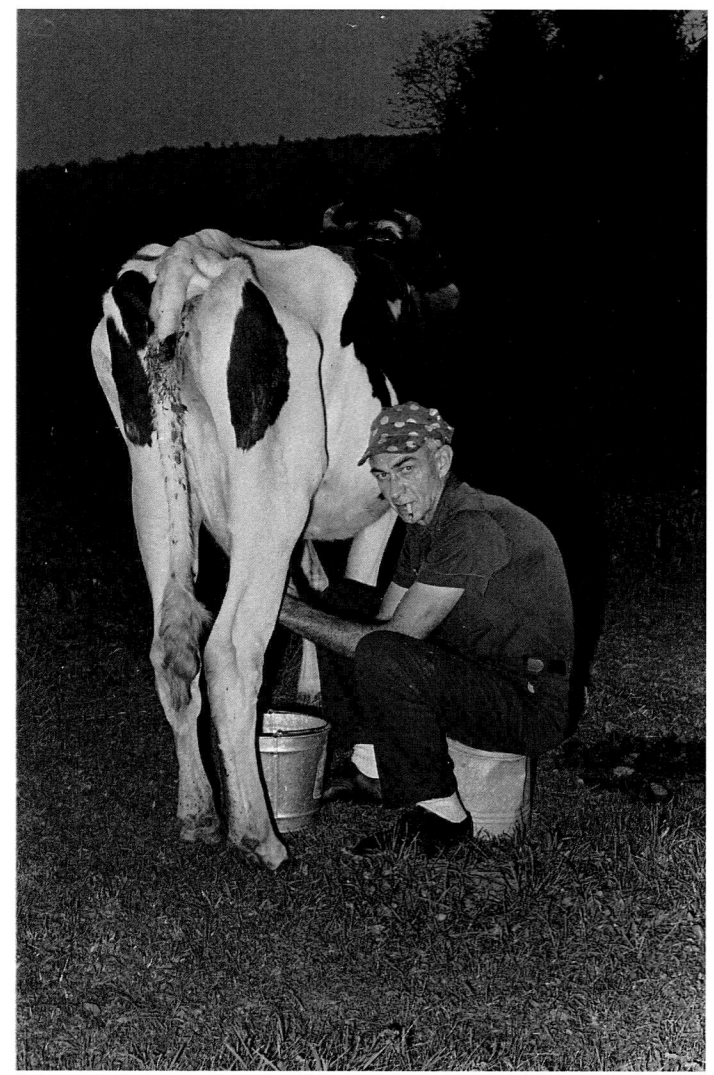

Milking a cow in the pasture, just about dark. October 1973.

something over 3.5%. Queenpin was sold in the summer of 1978 to Amelio Curti of Tulare, California who wanted to use her for super ovulation (where fertilized eggs are taken from top drawer cows and implanted into the uterus of cows of lesser heritage for gestation). But something happened, and Queenpin died in California in December 1978. She came with an excellent background: her sire (and Patches' maternal grandsire) was Whirlhill Kingpin, one of the best bulls ever at the Northeast Breeders Association (NEBA), now Sire Power, stationed in Tunkhannock. Her dam, Cherry Acres Barbara was daughter of Ron Hembury's first 4-H calf, from the Clayton Sharpe farm in Wyoming County. Top line bulls on the paternal side pedigree of Patches were her sire Round Oak Rag Apple Elevation, and her grandsire Tidy Burke Elevation, another top bull at Sire Power. Both bulls have produced outstanding daughters for dairy farmers throughout northeastern Pennsylvania. The All-Elevation Sale at Turlock on October 26th listed Patches as Lot No. 2, consigned by the Patches Syndicate; she was sold to Heidi Betschart of Modesto, California, for $6100. Our thanks to our far west reporter, to Merlin Carlson, and to the Hemburys for supplying pictures and information about Cherry Acres Patches Elevation, subject of the Holstein Cow Affair.

*The Sullivan Review*, November 21, 1979, p. 16.

# Section
# 6

*Dushore Borough and
Around the County*

van Revi

MORNING, FEBRUARY 24, 1983

Eddie Moll with his pet rooster. Only a boy on
a farm knows the joy and pleasure of owning a
pet rooster. *The Sullivan Review*, July 18, 1974, p. 1.

## Big Downtown Dushore Fire Was Six Years Ago Today

Today, January 26, 1989, is the sixth anniversary of the fire. I was awakened around 3 a.m. by the phone in my hotel room in Philadelphia, where I was attending the annual conference of veterinarians at the University of Pennsylvania. I quickly dressed, checked out of the hotel and headed home in the little '79 Ford Fiesta. It was the longest trip I've ever made from Philly. Top speed for the little car was about 55 mph. Just about daylight I came into Dushore and saw the old fire hall still standing. Everything was gone on the south side of Main Street from The Sullivan Review building to the red light. Those Dushore firemen did a great job saving the fire hall and The Sully, and for this we are still appreciative. As I wandered around town, I hoped someone was taking pictures, as I didn't have a camera at the time. Our news editor then was Leayn Stockdill of Laporte. "Will we get a paper out today?" she asked. It was Wednesday, go-to-press day. "We'll try," I said. With all the equipment out of The Sully building–it had been carried across the street to Dehler's Decorating & Paint Store–we didn't know exactly how it would be done. Well, Francis Hochberg performed some magic with the electricity in the other Sully building (the former McDonald building), we moved the typesetter there and got to work. We had to make some phone calls, but several lines were out in Dushore so Stevie (Mrs. Shoemaker) and I went to the Shady Nook in New Albany to place some calls. The gals at The Shady Nook treated us to breakfast. Bob McGuire came in and processed a few rolls of film, made screened prints for the paper to be published that day. Some good color shots of the blaze were taken by John Hoodak's sons and Bill Bohensky, Jr. It's a wonder more buildings didn't burn. I had a call later from a friend in Tunkhannock who asked what was going on in Dushore. I told her The Sully didn't burn because it was "sanctified." Joe Lynch, a native of Dushore, remarked that he'd waited all his life for the town to have a fire like this and he slept through it. The paper was out on time, on the street Thursday morning, thanks to all of the staff and the people in town who helped.

*The Sullivan Review*, January 26, 1989, p. 2.

Dushore trestle with a Lehigh Valley steam engine. 1948. The track was laid around 1871 when the line was extended to Bernice and Mildred; the trestle was dismantled in the mid 1950s.

## Ralph

Veteran staff member and contributor to *The Sullivan Review*, Ralph the basset hound, died Friday, March 11, 1983 after a lingering illness. Toward the end only her spirit, her weakly wagging tail and a remnant of her resonant voice remained, no more walks about town visiting her favorite spots. In May 1972 son Mike, then a student at Wilkes College, had to buy a dog for his girl friend; he visited a litter of basset hounds at the Arthur Edkin farm between Point Bethel and Deer Lake and chose Ralph. But then the girl friend couldn't keep the puppy where she lived, so Ralph, a female named for a lady carpenter on the TV program "Green Acres," moved to Dushore. As a young dog she tended to run, once going half way to Wyalusing. She had a baying bark like a coonhound, and could be located by her distinctive voice. She eventually established a beat, first thing in the morning heading to Mrs. Baumunk's for an Archway cookie (brand was important). Meandering down the hill, she avoided the Agway during business hours–she was afraid of "Steady Eddie" McMahon–and cruised around the Super Duper lot before giving a few barks to get into The Sully office. She greeted everyone with a bay, accepted any offers of Milk Bone treats, then went up the circular stairway to her sleeping bag on the second floor. She would come down when she heard familiar voices, sometimes following favorite people around town. She took her good-natured time crossing streets, traffic slowing down or stopping to accommodate her. She enjoyed riding in an automobile and watching the scenery. After the downtown fire destroyed familiar buildings, she couldn't get her bearings; she no longer climbed the circular stair, wagged her tail vigorously or sounded her distinctive voice. She will be remembered through her many photographs and the enjoyment she brought to family and friends.

*The Sullivan Review*, March 17, 1983, p. 6.

## Dushore Borough Figures for 1987

With the federal government tossing around figures like the trillion dollar deficit, the Persian Gulf activities bringing the true cost of oil to about $140 a barrel, the Postal Service about to lose millions because Congress won't ante up the "revenue forgone" (postal subsidies), the aver-

van Review

Thursday Morning September 16, 1976    Single Copy 25¢

Ralph the basset hound waits in vain for her friends who are now in high school or off to college. The street is quiet, the sun is warm, so why not take a nap?

Ralph the basset hound.

Ralph anticipating breakfast in the kitchen. January 12, 1978.

age citizen is helpless to do much about the situation. At the grass roots level, in Dushore Borough, for example, things might not be much different. Last week we decided to find out how far "in the hole" Dushore Borough had slipped over the past few years. When added up, it came to $852,903 not counting proposed projects such as repairs to the creek wall along Water Street and a new bridge across the creek on Center Street. If you consider the borough's population between 680 and 700 persons, then each would owe about $1200 of this sum. How did we arrive at this figure? We included all aspects of the borough's operation: the fire company, the sewer authority, the water company, and borough government. After all, the money must come from all of the people at sometime or another. Example: the remaining sewer authority obligation after installation of the system in 1976 is $471,877. The fire hall mortgage is $57,000 on the building and $10,000 on the new roof; the water company owes $51,526 on various projects (reservoir and Carpenter Street line); the balance on the water line installed on German Street at the time the sewer was installed is $85,500 (payment of $1500 is due every six months); the borough has to (or soon will) borrow $117,000 to pave the streets, $60,000 to buy and refurbish a borough office building. Add these up: total is $852,903. True, some of the obligations are self-amortizing, such as the sewer loan (40 years) and the water company debts.

Don't get lost – follow the signs.

But streets, buildings, bridges and walls are not self-amortizing. Proposed projects such as the creek wall and the Center Street bridge could easily add another $200,000 to the total. And the fire company is now looking for $90,000 to buy a new truck to sustain its capacity to protect the town and maintain the local fire insurance rating. What regulates the borough's borrowing capacity? According to the Borough Code, a borough may incur obligations up to 250 per cent of its borrowing base, the average of receipts for the last three fiscal years times 250%. For Dushore Borough, receipts in 1984 were $116,611; 1985, $121,403; 1986, $197,026, an average of $140,675. This times 250% is $351,687 or the allowable borough debt. If one takes the total of obligations figure of $852,903, and subtracts self-amortizing obligations of $608,903, the actual borough indebtedness at this time is $244,000. This leaves a cushion of $107,687 for additional borough borrowing. Who said the federal government is the only one with big figures? *The Sullivan Review*, July 2, 1987, p. 6.

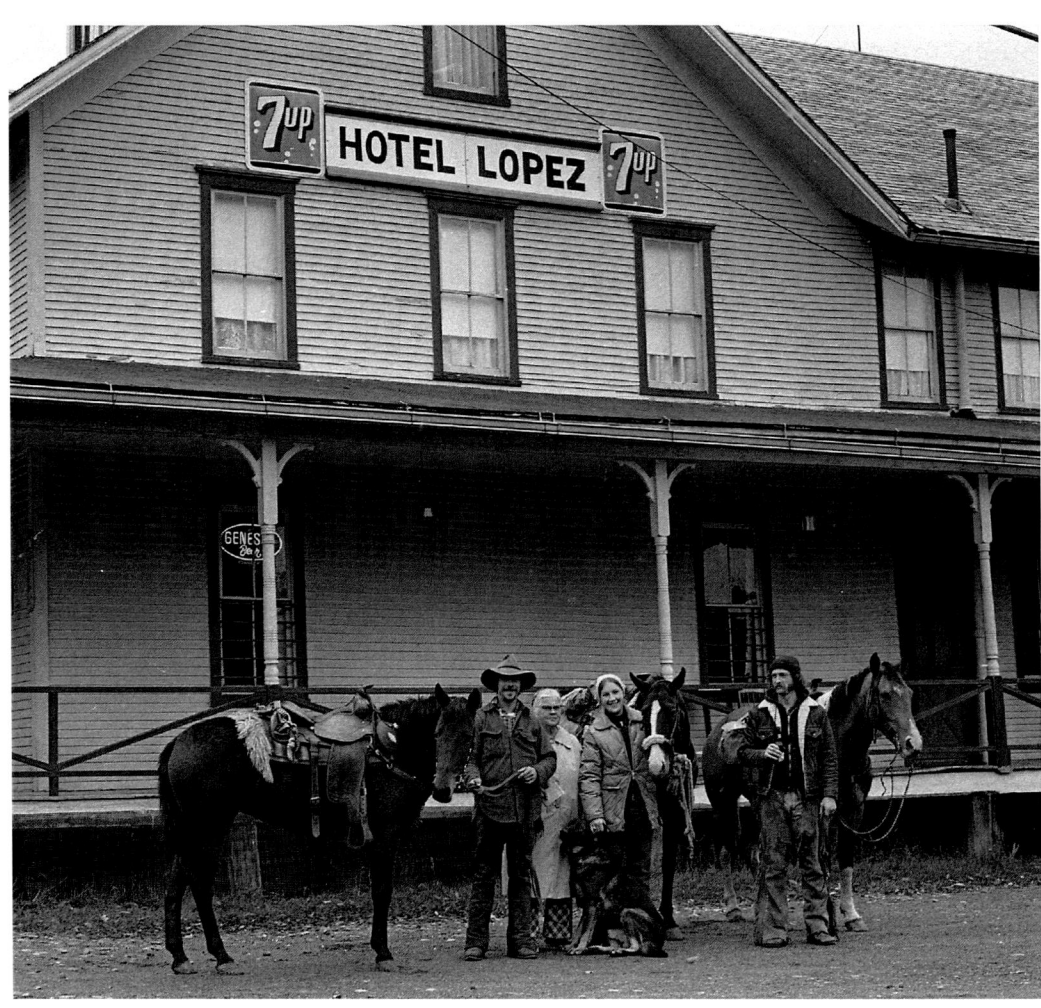

Trail riders stopped at Hotel Lopez before heading over Dutch Mountain. Mrs. Edith Shuman, behind the dog, stabled the horses. October 13, 1977.

Trail horse in Lopez. October 13, 1977.

## On Being a County Commissioner, 1980-1984

I was elected county commissioner in the general election of November 1979 and took office in January 1980 with fellow commissioners Maynard Reibson and John Potuck. Others filling out the row offices were Alice Taylor, treasurer; Clair Johnson, recorder, clerk and prothonotary; Doug Karge, sheriff. The chief clerk was Pam Kravitz and Kathy Robbins was deputy chief clerk. The commissioners met officially one day a week, which gave us time to keep other jobs; Reibson worked on his farm and Potuck ran his furniture store. Routine County operations were carried on by the chief clerk. Our salary was set by the state at $14,000 for commissioners of eighth class counties, up from $8,000 for the previous board. The County solicitor was K.B. Lee, who never came to a meeting unless called. The only regular visitor was Harry Dietrick, who represented a citizen activist group and was determined to get the state to pay more in lieu of taxes for state owned land. The four-year term was an education in itself.
*The Sullivan Review*, 1989.

## New Faces in the County, Summer 1978

During the last 10 years [1968-1978] we have noticed that the population of Sullivan County is changing–many new folks moving in, some "older" residents moving out. It means getting acquainted with new faces, new names and new occupants of familiar properties. With this in mind, we went "up and down" the county, checking out the business places that are new or under new management. The list is amazing. Before we go any further, please note this disclaimer: our apologies if a business is missed, it's not intentional. Let us know and we'll cover it next time. At the southern end of the county at Strawbridge along Route 220 there's a new store called Katie's Country Store, a friendly shop with some new ideas in merchandising. Going north into Muncy Valley, you'll come to St. Clair's Agway Store; nearby you can meet the new owners of the Valley Inn. Continuing north, you'll pass McHenry's Sub Shop, also known as Maizie's. At Sonestown, you'll find a much enlarged grocery and general store operated by Ed Houseknecht and his wife. They have a new front on what used to be a plain cinder block building. Along 220 where Muncy St. comes in, the Pine Tavern is now operated by Frank Frederick. If you need fuel for the car, you can get it at Botsford's station, just below Laporte on Route 220. When you get to Laporte, don't get confused in this smallest county seat–ask directions from Joe at the Courthouse. He'll tell you where Frances Fiester and June Brandt have their antique shops. If Joe isn't around, ask Leo McMahon at the Red and White. Headed for Dushore?

PATZ automated feeding equipment delivers silage to feeding bunk. Probably an ad promo, 1969

99

On the way you'll pass the Rock Run Center that includes, among other things, a real estate office. Have a cup of coffee at Sally's "Springwater" at Foley's Corner. After a stop at Bartholomew's (formerly the Jan-Carol) for lunch, you can coast into Dushore, where you'll find many new faces: Stroud's Supply, Dehler's Decorating, Ron Calaman's Insurance, Blue Country Music Shop, Hutchinson Upholstery, and Harry the Fishman's shop, called Land and Sea. Also in Dushore these new businesses: Glendon Furniture, Radio Shack, Hochberg Plumbing, Minier's Corner Luncheonette, Karpovich's Garage, Grace Rekito's Barber Shop. Going north of town, you'll pass the Wagon Wheel florist and garden shop before you come to Rheem Textile, metal fabricators. Nearby is Black's Car-Wash. Back in Dushore, you may want to stop at the Green Swan, now under the management of Margaret and John Hoodak. Take a right on Main St. and you'll come to Widmann's, a store full of notions, potions and patents. The Medicine Shoppe, formerly on West Main, Dushore, moved this past year to a new building alongside Stroud's Supply. Stop in and see Jim or 'Lyn and their little-well, it's not really a bear hound, but it thinks it is. Later this summer, you'll find a coin-operated laundry along Route 220 opposite the park. You can sit on a park bench while you do your wash. Our survey of new businesses wouldn't be complete without going to Mildred, where we find J & J (Joe and John Strabryla) Outfitters, a sporting goods store, and the newly named Birch Creek Tavern, so named for the creek that runs through Mildred. Joe Wenner, Gerard Kaier and Ray Cox operate the service stations in Mildred; you can buy fuel or get mechanical and body repairs. Take a trip south to Route 87, beginning at the junction with Route 220. You can find Mary's Red Door; just beyond is Dushore Wood Products Co., a newly built, completely modern sawmill.

Proceeding toward Forksville there's Loyalsock Outfitters in a revitalized dairy barn. Great to recycle an old barn! Along the way south you'll pass the Millview Motel, under new management. Near here you'll find paved roads going up to Jim Chase's Farm and Wood Stove Service, and Dick McCarty's PATZ Farm Equipment. In Forksville, Walter Franki now owns and operates the store at the covered bridge. Go on toward Hillsgrove and you'll pass Gardner's Inn, formerly the Forksville Inn. Dennis Renninger now owns the store at Hillsgrove, where you can see a real country post office and buy a stamp. No trip around Sullivan County would be complete without a visit to Eagles Mere. New owners and new shops blossom every summer. For starters, the Eagles Mere Inn, owned by the Bob Olivers has a cozy lounge with original wall paintings. Then there's Lund's Village Store Emporium next to an interesting general store. The Sweet Shoppe across the street is just that and serves summer luncheons. Also in the neighborhood, the Fashion Sport Shop of Moyer and Worthington and the Health Food Store owned by Joan Wright. In case you're not aware, there are two art shops in Eagles Mere: Hendl's on Laporte Ave. and Berry's across the street from the bank. Mention should be made of the Lake Shore Inn, now operated by the Houzouris family and featuring a traditional European cuisine. This about completes the list of new faces and new places in Sullivan County.

*The Sullivan Review Tourist Guide*, May 18, 1978, p. 14.

Harrington and Co. Creamery, German Street, Dushore. Opened in 1907, the Creamery used local dairies
to produce condensed milk, powdered milk and Dolly Madison ice cream; it closed in the early 1970s.

## Can You Remember These Dushore Landmarks?

I keep telling my patients and their owners, friends and associates, "Don't get old." Somebody asked how do you know if you're getting old? For starters, you're getting old if you can remember some of these old landmarks: the locomotive and cars rumbling over the trestle in Dushore; the A&P Store on the corner of Main and German Streets in downtown Dushore; the steam whistle at the Harrington & Co. Creamery (when it sounded, provided the wind was right, you could hear it in Colley). If you can remember the smoke stack at the creamery, you might recall all of the trucks in town carrying milk in 40 quart cans. Can you remember the GLF, predecessor of the Dushore Agway and the adjoining Flynn Lumber Yard, later the Dushore Car Co. where old trolley cars were restored? Can you remember buying a bushel of clams in a burlap sack for $20 at the A&P, or going to Ralph Rohe's Red & White Market next to the Dushore Post Office on German Street? You might be older than you think if you can remember chicken feed in printed cotton bags that your mother made into a dress or an apron. You might even recall, if you are old enough, when there was a chicken farm or two within the borough

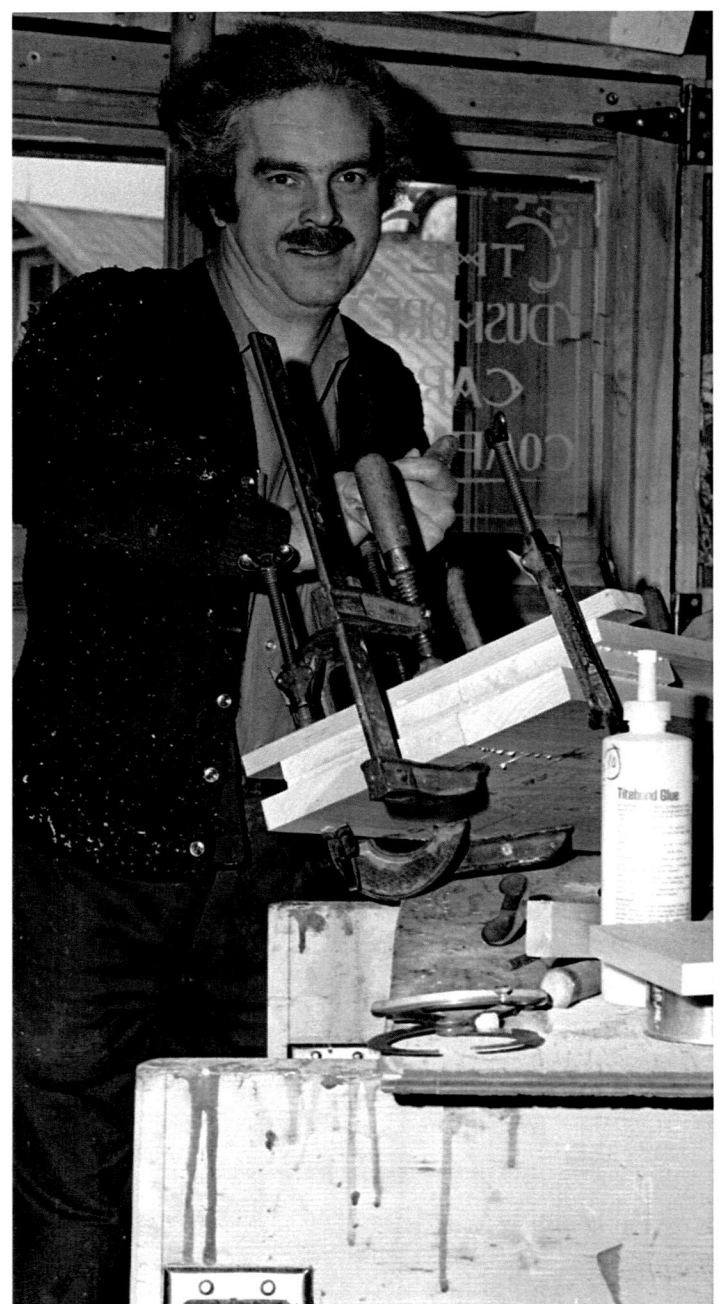

Ed Blossom, master craftsman of the Dushore Car Company, restored old light rail trolleys in the 1970s in the building that is now Dushore Agway. March 3, 1977

Top: "801" car on blocks

Bottom: Front end of the "801." January 1976

Top: Restoring the interior of the "801." 1976

Bottom: Blackpool boat car heads up Railroad Street to the Dushore Car Co. 1975. The car was shipped from England to be refitted in Dushore and sent to Philadelphia.

limits–Soutos (on the site of the Jerry Frank residence) and Joe Obert's, past the railroad station on the right; just out of town, Don Green's (he helped start the chicken barbecue business), where he raised pullets by the hundreds. I remember Art Rohe plowing snow off the borough streets with a John Deere tractor engine. And before no-till farming, County Agent Bill Gregory had a contest to see which farmer could turn the best furrow. Winter storms might test your memory. Remember when PennDOT waited until the storm was over to start plowing the roads, resulting in a lot of snow bound plows? Miles of snow fences were erected every fall to capture blowing snow. You are old if you also remember putting chains on the rear wheels of your car or truck, or even having a set in the car just in case. With the snow gone in early spring, county residents of a certain age will remember mud roads and sink holes, and carrying a bumper jack to lift a wheel out of a deep rut. And one more thing–I can remember making the first track on Route 87 from Dushore to Forksville after a new snowfall. Now, it's your turn.

*The Sullivan Review* Tourist Guide, Fall/Winter, 2007.

## On Paper vs. Electronic Ballots, May 1982

A recent editorial aired on a regional TV program suggested the elimination of paper ballots in the election process and suggested an electronic alternative. Of course, the editorialist spent most of his two minutes on the advantages of electronic voting, of which there are many, suggesting in the meantime that rural communities get with the trend and do something about old-fashioned slow paper ballots. So I prepared an answer, partly in fun but partly serious, as an elected official among whose duties are the conduction of elections. What? Do away with paper ballots? Take all the fun out of life for the local election boards? Reduce to electronics the last vestige of American election process, removing the suspense of who won what office until 8:05 p.m.? What would television do for the remainder of the evening? Analyze? And what about the few dollars the county election boards pay the various inspectors and judges? That's like taking candy from a baby and giving it to an electronic monster to eat in a few moments of digital time. Our election boards, when not standing that 13-hour or more stint on election day, are busy at other jobs, from homemaking to making ends meet. But the electronic machine works two days out of the year, then sits idly by, collecting dust, getting out of sync, requiring maintenance, and taking up storage space, besides adding responsibility to the county election boards–which they could no doubt handle, but would rather not. It's enough for them to inventory collapsible voting booths. There's something about a pencil–it's cost effective, needs little maintenance, is cheap to buy and doesn't scare the voters. There is merit in requesting speed on election day, but every time these new machines take over you lose a lot of grass roots participation, be it voting, collecting taxes or preparing duplicates. We do need more interest in elections, don't we? The bottom line in rural counties is how the cost of the equipment, which would be used fewer than 30 hours per year, can be justified considering the numbers of voters who regularly come out to vote. When it gets to costs, Sullivan County spent $5,800 in last week's primary election, with little error–(one vote less for Bonner, one vote more for Manherz)–very likely less than the cost of one machine (and we would need 15). I think there are still millions of people throughout the USA who like to sit down and read all about it in their local newspapers, the day after election.

*The Sullivan Review*, May 27, 1982, p. 11.

## Some Election Reflections, November 1999

The 1999 General Election is history. Some good people won. And some good people lost. Real politicians will dismiss thoughts of this election and get on with preparing for their next campaign. In Sullivan County the new method of counting votes revealed some interesting facts. Take the Commissioners race, the only local one in which there was a contest. The two top vote getters were separated by only 11 votes, while the third highest trailed by 172 and the fourth by 402 votes. What the vote counting machine showed was that more than 500 voters "over voted," that is, they voted for three commissioner candidates instead of two as directed on the ballot. For some reason "over voting" is a problem in commissioner elections. In Bradford County and in Lycoming County, well over a thousand voters "over voted" in each county. The principal reason is that voters don't read ballot instructions. "Vote for only 2," or "Elect 2," the ballot may read. If more than two are selected, the votes for commissioner are not counted. Another reason is that there is no party (Republican or Democratic) organization that endeavors to instruct voters about this. Local committee persons are virtually non-existent. The number of "over votes" could have easily changed the complexion of the Commissioners race for the top vote getters and may also have helped the low vote getter. There is a reason for voting "only for two" in commissioner elections: vote for two and the election results will always yield a minority commissioner, so that each of the two parties is represented. But there are exceptions to this, too: when a write-in candidate wins over those listed on the ballot, a county could end up with three commissioners from the same political party. This happened not too many years

Don't forget to Vote!

ago in Bradford County, when three Republicans were elected to office. So, every vote counts. Your vote is important at any time. Remember the last congressional election when Don Sherwood beat Pat Casey by some 500 votes? One more vote from each of the 500 districts in the 10th Congressional District could have elected Pat Casey instead of Don Sherwood. You can bet your boots that Mr. Casey is getting ready for the next congressional election and that Don Sherwood is also getting ready to meet his opponent. That's why we always say you can't second guess an election anymore than you can second guess a cow.

*The Sullivan Review*, November 18, 1999, p. 5.

## Carl S. Driscoll (1916-2007) and
## Sullivan County High School

Carl S. Driscoll, 90, was the man who brought the present Sullivan County school system into being from a collection of rural high schools to the centralized high school of today. A farm boy who walked from his Forks Township home a mile or so to the one room school at Campbellsville, he went on to become superintendent of Sullivan County school system, then chief executive of Intermediate Unit 17, a consortium of regional school districts. Carl Driscoll, along with John Fiorini, the first principal at the new high school, saw to it that the school building would be "state of the art." The school boards of each high school (Cherry Township, Sullivan Highlands and Loyalsock) were consolidated into the nine-member board we have now, and it was Carl Driscoll who made the consolidation work. He essentially conducted the board meetings, asking the members, "What is your pleasure?" When he got mad it was not for long. In one instance he got so mad at a board member he told him to leave; the member left and never returned to complete his term. Carl Driscoll was a respected "boss" by all on the teaching staff and was always ready to help when needed. He was always a teacher. When the present high school was built, a big discussion concerned what type of floors would be put down in the hallways. The terrazzo floor was the final decision; as a further note, chewing gum was prohibited lest it would mar the floor. On a recent visit to the school the hallway floors looked as new today as they did in 1963.

*The Sullivan Review*, January 24, 2007, p. 16.

Sullivan County High School District 4 basketball champs, 1976
Griffins sports are popular winter entertainment in the County.

## Read Across America

Every year the National Education Association sponsors a nationwide reading event called "Read Across America." It celebrates the joys of reading and honors Dr. Seuss (Theodore Geisel) whose birthday is next Sunday, March 2. Research shows that the more children read, the better they read, and the more they read outside of school, the better they do in school. Sullivan County students are becoming better readers, as they have advanced in regional reading competitions for elementary and junior high school students. Good readers make better writers, as evidenced by students' writing contributions to The Sully's annual Tourist Guides and Christmas supplements. While many forms of mass communication exist today that do not require reading, such as television and musical incantations, there's more pleasure to be had in reading books, magazines, and, of course, newspapers. As Confucius said, "Writing makes an exact man; conference makes a ready man; and READING makes a full man." Thanks for reading *The Sullivan Review* and this week's "Satterfield Flyer."
*The Sullivan Review*, February 27, 2003, p. 11.

## School Bus Dilemma

With the Sullivan County School Board facing an almost one million dollar school bus transportation cost in 2008, it might be time to recall when there were no school buses. Consider that at one time there were 95 one-room schools in the county; almost all pupils and teachers walked to school. One teacher I knew, the late Ella Rouse, lived in Albany Valley, about four miles from Dushore. She walked to her one room school located near Kinsley's Corners in Cherry Township and back every day, a distance of seven miles. She likely had to build the fire in the schoolhouse when she got there. So, with the cost of mandated bus transportation, it appears there is no easy way out. Perhaps consolidation of a couple of routes might help. The centralized school, miles from most homes, precludes walking. Does anyone have any ideas?
*The Sullivan Review*, April 9, 2008, p. 7. [original title, "School Bus Story"]

## Doc's message to the class of 2006

June is the season for graduations and commencement addresses. A few nights ago when I couldn't fall asleep, I thought of how commencement speeches often bring on the sandman. Although few remember the advice given at these exercises, I recall three things from my high school graduation 67 years ago, in June 1939, from West Pittston High School in Luzerne County. There were 177 seniors in my class. When I walked up on stage the superintendent, Mr. R.J.W. Templin, called out my entire name–Thomas William Hatfield Shoemaker, Junior–and the audience laughed at the idea that someone in the class had five names. Now, of course, my name is "Doc," hardly anyone knows my given names. My third remembrance is that Willis Netter, a fellow senior, and I played an instrumental duet–Willie on the tuba and T.W.H.S. on the piccolo. We played the classic, "Elephant and the Fly." We had practiced it for months, and the audience cheered. Now, senior classmen, it's your turn to remember something of your graduation night–out on the lawn by the high school in summer weather, while hope for the future abounds.

What changes high school curricula have seen over the last 67 years: our shop class used hand tools, saws and planes, and we sharpened chisels on a whetstone to complete a simple woodworking project. We carried our lunch.

One-room school, Campbellsville, Forks Township

Now classrooms have computers and other state-of-the-art equipment, libraries include resources on the Internet, classrooms are well lighted and meals come from in-house cafeterias. Did I go to high school in the dark ages? Hardly. I always come back with the remark that those who developed the atom bomb were trained in one-room school houses, figuratively to be sure. The first graduating class from the present Sullivan County High School was in June 1964. I was one of the teaching staff, and principal John E. Fiorini assigned everyone to do something. The school hired a professional speaker for the occasion, Imre Kovacs, a Hungarian educator from New York City, whose big concern was that he had to return to Manhattan immediately after the ceremony. Transporting him fell to me, so around 9:00 p.m., in a downpour, we left for New York City.

Riding along in my 1960 T-bird was Don Chubbuck, also on the teaching staff. We didn't get lost. I wish the class of 2006 smooth sailing, but make your own way, do your own thing; above all, continue your education, and strive to do your best. *Auf wiedersehen*.

## Forksville "Arrival"

A favorite pastime of ours is working crossword puzzles, not only in *The Sullivan Review* but also those found in the Daily and Sunday editions of *The New York Times*. We don't pretend to be experts; seldom are the puzzles completed before the next one arrives, and even then some clues elude the imagination. We have heard that the appearance of one's name in the *Times* puzzles means that national recognition or notoriety has been achieved. In short, you have "arrived," when the clue points to you, or your town. Last week when working a *Times* puzzle around bedtime, this clue popped up: "Red of Forksville, PA." Of course, we knew immediately who it was–Red Grange–a Forksville native and very much deserving of six squares in any crossword. Howard Edward "Red" Grange was a half back for the University of Illinois and the Chicago Bears; he was in the College and Pro football Halls of Fame, MVP of the Big Ten in 1924 and named best college football player of all time by ESPN in 2008 (Wikipedia, August 15, 2014). There you are, Forksville–immortality in a *New York Times* crossword puzzle. Incidentally, crosswords have been appearing in the United States since Dec. 21, 1913, when newspaperman Arthur Wynne put the first one on a Sunday page of *The New York World* as a filler. From then on puzzles became standard fare in newspapers and magazines all over the world except in the Orient, where language characters don't lend themselves to vertical and horizontal arrangement. One quote: "The crossword puzzle was America's favorite licit indoor activity in the days before television"–(*Publishers Weekly*). Experts contend that crosswords help maintain words in the language, and certainly help the vocabularies of those who work them. They cost little but time to work, and give one a feeling of accomplishment when a word is filled in. Recently, the new national daily newspaper *USA Today* began including a puzzle–after *The Sullivan Review* wrote to them and said their image could be improved by including a crossword–and by golly, it was!
*The Sullivan Review*, December 16, 1982. p. 14.


## Summer Concerts at Eagles Mere, 1987

"The hills were alive with music" last weekend, with the presentation of two outstanding concerts sponsored by the Eagles Mere Friends of the Arts at the David A. DeWire Center in Eagles Mere. A standing room only crowd was on hand Saturday night to hear two hours of pure jazz, much of it improvised, by seven artists. As always, not a

note of music was in evidence; if there was any direction from Derf Nolde, piano, or Ed Polcer, cornet, it was a knowing glance, a quick hand movement, or a step away from the microphone. The music appealed to the ear, and the rhythm appealed to the foot. Spontaneous applause followed individual interpretations of the songs being played. Others rounding out the Ambassadors of Jazz were Tom Artin on trombone, Barry Rank on banjo, DeWitt Kay on bass, John Weber on clarinet and Al (Mr. Time) DeGeorge on drums. All are soloists in their own right, and together they produced one of the most entertaining shows I've attended–for $5, the one low price established by the Friends of the Arts. Who said there's nothing to do in Sullivan County? For this concert in Wilkes-Barre, you'd pay $20, $40 in New York City if you could get a seat. We hope they'll return next summer to Eagles Mere. Then on Sunday evening, the well-known, precise and polished Philadelphia Trio presented selections of classical music appealing to a different set of ears, with rhythm limited to the wiggle of one's big toe. In this concert, Barbara Sonies, violin, presented three numbers in rag time syncopation, accompanied by Elizabeth Keller, piano. These were a delightful diversion from their usual program. The third member of the Trio, Deborah Reeder, cellist, proved again the instrument's need and ability to complete the tonal qualities of the selections. The Philadelphia Trio was formed in 1971 and makes several appearances each summer in Eagles Mere. It has recorded two albums, toured European cities, conducted workshops throughout the United States and made frequent radio appearances. The community is fortunate to have the talents of these fine musicians each summer, and the Eagles Mere Friends of the Arts are to be complimented on their selection of programs.
*The Sullivan Review*, July 16, 1987, p. 10.

## Lucky Number in Eagles Mere

Now, I'm not a gambler, or a fan of the lottery, the numbers, the horses, or the sweepstakes. But consider the following. Last week, on December 30th, I was asked to attend the opening of Evergreen Lodge at Eagles Mere. The building, once part of the Crestmont Inn, was restored with modern facilities and new furniture by Mr. and Mrs. Bob Oliver of Eagles Mere. Since I had in my effects an old room key medallion from the original Crestmont Inn, I decided to give it to the Olivers as a house-warming gift. I had purchased the medallion several years ago, on the day Crestmont Inn furnishings were auctioned off. The medallion was a sunburst disc about two inches in diameter,

CRESTMONT INN, EAGLES MERE, PA.

The Crestmont Inn on Hurricane Hill, old 1930s postcard from Eagles Mere

solid brass and embossed with "Crestmont Inn–Eagles Mere, PA, place in any mailbox if carried away." It was numbered Room 222. I shined it all up, and when I gave it to Bob I said casually, "Bob, you should play that number." Bob showed his gift around the group; when his older daughter saw it she exclaimed, "Dad, that's the duplicate of the one hanging above my dresser at home! Room 222!" All the more reason to "play that number." On Tuesday night as I glanced through the *Williamsport Sun*, the lottery results on page 5 caught my eye. Guess what number won on New Year's Eve–the day after I gave Bob the medallion? Why, 222! It was the largest payout the state lottery had ever made and actually threw it into the hole for that day. A fellow never knows, does he?
*The Sullivan Review*, January 7, 1982, p. 7.

## Middendorf Home Fire, New Year's Eve, Early 1950s

As I write the obituaries of people I have personally known, I often recall some event that occurred while I visited their farm or home. Such was the case this week as I wrote about Mary Middendorf, and the following story came to mind. It was New Year's Eve in the early 1950's, around three in the afternoon. I was returning to Dushore from a farm call at Cummisky's on Marsh Road. As I approached the Middendorf home, I could see evidence of a chimney fire–smoke under pressure billowing out of the chimney. Knowing they didn't have a telephone, I stopped to see if I could help. Vince, Mary's brother, was in the kitchen and had the kitchen stove pipe pulled away from the chimney. The inside of the chimney looked like the mouth of a blast furnace, with a roar associated with a blowtorch. He was holding a quart sized dipper in his right hand and with his left was splashing water into the inferno. The water, vaporizing, made the burning more intense. I said to Vince, "Shall I run to town and call the fire company?" "Let's see how it looks in the attic," he said. So, Vince went out the door, walked, did not run, to the barn and returned with a ladder. We went upstairs, placed the ladder under the trap door and got into the attic. Fortunately, the chimney was sound. Back downstairs, I again told Vince the fire company should be called. "Wait 'til I ask Mary," he said, and getting a "Yes, go ahead," I sped into town. The Dushore Fire Chief at the time was Art Yonkin, who was employed at Fitzpatrick and Lambert, the Ford Garage. I found Art and told him of the dilemma. Art said he'd have to sound the fire alarm, then the steam whistle on the creamery. Among the firemen responding was the late Jim Schoch, who climbed up the ladder (outside the house) and did a job on the chimney fire.

*The Sullivan Review*, February 25, 1993, p. 13.

Heavy snows on trees

Fresh eggs for sale

## Deserted Downtown, Winter 2005 in Sullivan County

With the February 28-March 1 snowstorm dumping six to eight inches of flakes, things came to a standstill in town. The C&N Bank didn't open until 9:30, but M&T opened on schedule. Traffic was minimal. One could walk diag-onally under the red light from the Jolly Trolley to M&T without getting run over. Roy Cox came in from his home on the Horseshoe to report the snowfall to folks at the Jolly Trolley. He predicted that spring might come. Anastasia McMahon Farrell stopped in for coffee and a bag of bird-seed, noting that her feeder was empty, no feed, no birds. *The Sullivan Review*, March 3, 2005, p. 11.

Bending trees, snow near deserted
downtown Dushore

# Section 7

*Outdoors in the Endless Mountains*

van Revi

Kayaking the Loyalsock. Annual white-water races were popular in spring in the 1970s and 1980s during high water in the Loyalsock.

## Snow

Thirty-seven years ago this month (February 1952) the Shoemakers moved to Dushore, and 1989 is the first year that I recall we didn't have a good measure of snow. Some years it was scant, but by mid-February there was always snow. Experts tell us this winter is not really unusual. The degree-days are about normal. No doubt about it, there's a shortage of precipitation, either snow or rain. We have two or more months remaining that can bring substantial snowfall. The blessing is, snow won't last as long with the lengthening days and moderate temperatures. I remember one snowy night in 1957 or 1958. About 8:00 I got a call from Joe McEneany to attend to a sick cow. Joe lived (and still does, though he's retired) on the Shaffer Notch Road, off Marsh Road toward Wyalusing, about eight miles from Dushore. But that road was drifted shut, so I set up a detour route, going north on 87 to Jake Kneller's, then cutting across the Dushore-Wyalusing road past Ambrosius's farm, Kauffman's and Huffman's. This road was open, though drifting was apparent. Les Miller was the navigator. My '57 Ford wagon had a keel plate (put on to keep from knocking the plug out of the oil pan) that allowed it to plow a little snow. At the junction of Shaffer Notch Road and the Wyalusing road, I switched back toward McEneany's, and almost made it. Joe hooked his tractor on the grabs (welded on the front of the Ford for just such emergencies) and pulled me up the hill to the barn. Going home, I used the same route, and was probably the last car to make it from Wilmot to Route 87 that night. It was about midnight when I got home. Later I found out that the Wilmot to 87 road was so drifted it took three days before the road could be opened for an undertaker to move the body of a woman who had died on the night of the storm. Well, those days are gone forever, but the memories are still fresh. It isn't likely such incidents will happen again, mainly because most of the little farms and their elderly caretakers are no longer in operation. Nowadays, those remaining on farms are able to do much of their own emergency work, so the late night calls are not commonplace. So much for the changing climate.

*The Sullivan Review*, February 9, 1989, p. 5.

## Down the Loyalsock With Canoe and Camera

Over the many years I've travelled up and down Route 87 between Hillsgrove and Montoursville, I've observed how placid the Loyalsock Creek looks. I often wished I had

Canoeists on the Loyalsock. March, 1983

Loyalsock pool, November 19, 1987

Looking toward Sonestown covered bridge, low water in Muncy Creek. August 29, 1991

time to make the trip downstream in a canoe. That time came last Sunday. Around 9:30 a.m. we put two canoes in the creek at the iron bridge north of Hillsgrove and headed downstream, fully committed to going as far as Montoursville, where we would be picked up in late afternoon. The day was bright; the clear, cold water sparkled and reflected the sun into our eyes. In rifts, we soon found it difficult to discern rocks hidden under the waves, and after the first half mile we found out how cold was the water. Manning the canoes were Laporte Mayor Robert (Bob) Carpenter and Bill Boatman in a fiberglass skimmer, and Doc Shoemaker and Bob Dufner in a 1925 vintage wooden canoe covered with fiberglass, very heavy, and equipped with a keel strip. I mention the keel mainly because it is something you can do without in waters such as the Loyalsock, where fast turns are more necessary than a keel will allow. What happened during the course of the next nine miles to Barbour's was due in great part to lack of maneuverability of the keel-equipped canoe. Our first misfortune, and the earliest spring time swim I ever recall, occurred when the front of the canoe jammed into the bank and couldn't be turned; the current carried the stern downstream and rolled us over. We recovered most everything and tied all loose equipment to the canoe. From then on, the camera was too wet to work. A mile downstream we stopped to eat a sandwich and put on dry socks. What a mistake. It turned out that was the only chance we had for lunch, because the canoe was flushed clean of everything on our next spill and the only thing holding the paddles was the upward pressure of the canoe against the tree we went under. We realized that while the Loyalsock looks calm and inviting from the road, once out of sight of pavement it is an invigorating, churning mass of white water at every turn in the valley. Tricky. By a stroke of luck, we recovered both paddles on this second spill and were able to continue downstream, but without lunch. By this time, Bob Carpenter had been laughing so much that his stomach muscles ached. He stood by while we baled out the water and laughed again. The next hour or so was uneventful except for the wind that blew up the Loyalsock Valley as if it were a wind tunnel, making it necessary to paddle harder. It was so strong that the Boatman and Carpenter canoe got sideways in the stream, was blown over and dumped. Bill's dollar cooler and a six-pack were lost on this dunking. It was our turn to laugh, but not for long. Going down a swift area, threading among seen and imagined stones, we hit one with a crack and were immediately thrown into the stream. I went clear of the canoe on one side; Bob Dufner hung on and made for the opposite shore with the canoe full of water. About 500 feet downstream we were able to get together again, each holding on to our paddles. My life vest was worth its weight in gold. By the time we had reached Barbour's, an overall drop of some 140 feet from Hillsgrove, we were ready to call it a day. We dried out a bit, got chocolate milk at Moore's store and waited for our car to take us home. Somehow, I gained two pounds during the day.

*The Sullivan Review*, May 8, 1980, p. 13

## Junk

When travelling about the County, or the country, this is the time of year when foliage doesn't obscure the unsightly side effects of civilization, namely junk cars, rusty iron or decayed buildings. None of us is immune to this scourge, which requires some elbow grease to clean out. So why not get at it? These things come about naturally, not always by intention. Materials get laid aside for future use–which never comes. So if you have a minute, an hour or a day, pick up the junk and get rid of it.

*The Sullivan Review*, May 3, 1979, p. 2.

## Trip Down the Loyalsock in the Flood of 2011

There's a story about a man travelling through Dushore and stopping by the red light to ask directions from a man sitting on the bench in front of the Jolly Trolley. In answer to the traveler's question, the old man on the bench said, "You can't get there from here." That was really the case last Wednesday and most of Thursday (September 7 and 8), when all main roads going through Sullivan County were closed due to flooding. Water

was flowing over the bridge at Ringdale; Route 220 north of New Albany was closed; Route 87 north to Mehoopany was closed; Route 87 south below Forksville and Hillsgrove was inundated. There was no way to get to Lopez, either, and dirt and gravel County roads were washed out. The rain just wouldn't stop. On Thursday afternoon we ventured out, went around a roadblock and ended up at Ringdale a few hours after water from the Loyalsock Creek poured over the bridge. Mrs. Joe McDonald was walking along Route 220 looking things over. The berm was washed out; in one spot water got under the pavement and lifted a piece off its base like a big pancake. She said she measured 15 ½" of rain. At the height of the storm, a mother and year old baby were evacuated from their home near the creek as the water was about to move the house off its foundation. It wasn't fit for occupancy when we looked at it. From Ringdale we went south on Route 87. The first thing we saw was Francis Moll's cornfield, flattened out and pressed to the ground by the rush of water. The Little

Loyalsock Creek roared by Cherry Mills Lodge, which was high and dry above a canyon. Farther down the road, a field of golden rod was combed flat, like the coat on a well-groomed dog. The road to the Shrimp Bridge at Rock Run was closed; we made no attempt to go there, because a turn around would have been impossible. All the way to Forksville, the creek knew no bounds, cleaning out anything that was loose. The large, flat field (maybe 50 acres) at the Brian McCarty farm was flooded extensively. No cattle in sight. He had recently sold his dairy cows and replaced them with a few feeders. Bridges were not covered by water where the Big Loyalsock and Little Loyalsock meet, since they are elevated enough to accommodate the flow. The Forksville covered bridge was also slightly higher than the water, because old timers knew how high to build a covered bridge. South of Forksville along Route 87 the floodwaters had completely eroded the berms, such that getting off the road would mean no shoulder to support your car. Debris of all sorts lined either side of the road

Duane Bacorn with trout

Chris Gessner with a nice trout
*The Sullivan Review*, April 18, 2002.

Rare shot of a porcupine climbing a tree. April 1971

where a few hours before there was only a river. Just north of Hillsgrove, water coming over a low spot took out the guide rail and heaved the pavement. We stopped to say "Hello" to postmaster Carol McElhaney at the Hillsgrove General Store; she told us Slab Run, on the edge of the Snell Brothers farm, flooded the cellar of her son's new house before washing out the lane from Route 87 to his property. At the south side of the village, water surrounded the Hillsgrove Hotel on its rush downstream—unbelievable floodwater, brown as the earth, covering any and all parcels of flatland. On the way home we met up with Julie Gavitt-Shaffer's donkey, which was rescued after a swim down the 'sock.

*The Sullivan Review*, September 14, 2011, p. 2.

## Porcupine Quills

Can you imagine on a warm spring night, in a sprinkle of rain, you let your dog out of the house for a bedtime run? Only, the dog doesn't come right back but instead shows up an hour later with a snout full of porcupine quills. This is what happened to Gene Richart's dog from Glen Mawr a few years ago. He called the doctor, who got out of bed, dressed and opened the office for the late night arrival. The big Labrador retriever, still wagging its tail but feeling sorry for himself, was sedated and put on the table for quill pulling. An hour later, the job was done. Gene looked at me and said, "He had 417 quills, I counted as you pulled them out." That's only a small number of the 30,000 quills a porcupine may have. And once removed, they grow back quickly. The fine, black tip of the quill is sharper than a nurse's needle, and to make a quill stick, hundreds of barbs on the stem help hold it in the victim's flesh. However, when the dog is sedated, the muscles of the skin relax and quills come out more easily. Porkys are loners. They are

scavengers, and given the chance will eat anything their sense of smell says might be good. Their sense of smell is perhaps 200 times that of a man. That's why, in Sullivan County, they frequent camps, summer cabins and cottages where a tasty morsel might be found. Porcupines are the second largest rodent in the country—the beaver is the largest—and are equipped with orange colored incisors, two upper and two lower, that can easily strip bark off a tree down to a juicy part of the trunk. One way to avoid a session with quills is to put a bell on your dog's collar to warn the porcupines—doesn't work all the time, but it helps. Another tip: if you have two or more dogs, only let one out at a time. For a complete resume of the porcupine, contact the Pennsylvania Game Commission at *www.pgc.state.pa.us*.

*The Sullivan Review*, May 4, 2011, p. 12.

## Bob Lambert's Porcupine Visitors

Readers of The Sully know that over the years a lot of stories and pictures have been published about our friendly ubiquitous Sullivan County porcupines. The latest porcupine caper comes from our friend Bob Lambert of the local Ford garage. It seems that porcupines are great scavengers, and when hungry will try most anything. Commonly, they approach a dog coop where they might find some unfinished dog food or a scrap from the table; the dog, sensing encroachment on his territory, tackles the porcupine with the usual results. But porcupines aren't restricted to edible leavings; they will also try something with a salty taste or a pheromone quality. Here's where friend Bob comes into the picture. In at least seven instances this year, the garage has had a call to come tow a car that has no brakes. You know, when you push the pedal to the floor and there's no resistance. With automatic transmissions, everything's coasting. Upon arrival at the garage mechanics find the car's hoses that carry the brake fluid to the brake cylinder completely chewed away, not just one hose to one wheel, but to all four wheels. The culprits: porcupines. They must like the salty taste of road weathered brake fluid hose or the chewy consistency of rubber or plastic or whatever; they get under cars, usually parked at a remote camp, and start nibbling. Adding insult to injury, the camper, fisherman or hunter has to walk to the nearest phone, call for help, and pay for it. Most auto insurance policies cover such things as broken windows, deer damage, and, now, according to one local insurance agent, porcupine damage. One thing about repairing auto brake hoses, compared to extracting quills from a dog's nose: you don't have to anesthetize a car and the mechanic generally doesn't get out of bed at 2 a.m. to fix the problem.

*The Sullivan Review*, July 14, 1988, p. 10.

## Bull Story

The expression often seen posted on walls of offices, including bar rooms and press-rooms, states that cows may come and cows may go but the bull goes on forever. The expression may have an element of truth. It seems that Mrs. Agnes Hochberg, who lives on Ringer Hill, sold her Hereford bull to Joe Scanlin, who lives in Forks Township west of the headwaters of Black Creek. The farms are about six miles apart by road, and directions on how to get from one to the other would confuse even a backpacker. The bull was trucked from the Hochberg farm to the Scanlin farm in the early evening about two weeks ago, and placed in the barnyard, supposedly secure behind the fence. What happened, no one knows, but the next morning when Mrs. Hochberg went to the barn to do chores, she was greeted by you-know-who, the Hereford bull. How he found his way back is a mystery, as the bovine has little homing instinct. With so much country between the two farms, confusing roads–including Route 87–other farms with cattle, steep hills, and all, it is remarkable that a Hereford could manage the return trip without the facilities of Ransom's Travel.

*The Sullivan Review*, July 20, 1978, p. 3.

## "Uncle Ed" Orlowski, One-Time Hunter

Chances to take pictures are often fleeting, as are chances to record voices. Events often pass before one realizes it's too late. Like summer in Sullivan County, gone before you can get used to it. I was reminded of these things on reading last week about the passing of Ed Orlowski of Mildred, whose stories, no matter how far fetched they sounded, would have made good recordings. Ed held forth quite often for the Wednesday night crowd at the Thunderbird Bar in Mildred, if not about his adventures while laying track in the mines around Bernice and Mildred, then about plowing snow drifts with a highway snowplow. But his greatest tale was his recollection of the one time he went hunting with friends on Dutch Mountain. One time, maybe two, he'd say, but that was it. It seems that, except for Ed, the roster was made up of experienced hunters; he was always placed on the least desirable stand, according to him, since he was dependent on his buddies for a sense of direction. In an old car, in the faint winter morning light, he proceeded across the mountain to the chosen place. The narrow road was rutted and muddy from late fall rains. Not frozen enough to support a vehicle. Ed was equipped with an unnamed deer rifle that he had said he knew how to shoot, but that he had never shot. His stand was at the edge of a clearing framed with barren huckleberry bushes, a little ways off the road. He waited and waited, finally heard a noise, a crashing sound coming toward him. There it was–a huge buck, 12 points, blinded by fear and bounding right toward him. A shot (not from Ed's gun) rang out and the deer lunged right at Ed, who ducked behind a tree just in time to avoid being run over. As he turned, the quarry was a white blur going through the bushes and Ed never got off a shot. Of course, it took a long time for Ed to live that down, since a

Richard Bahr of Dushore, left, with his 150-lb. bear taken in Forks Township. Right, Sherman Higley of Hillsgrove. *The Sullivan Review*, November 22, 1995, p. 1.

fellow hunter observed it from a nearby stand. More details appeared each time the story was told, but, according to Ed, that was the last time he ever went into the woods. As the senior member of the crowd, he held the title of "Uncle Ed;" when he talked everyone listened. Another story concerned the 16 boys of Mildred and Bernice who were all born in 1912 or 1913 and who were close pals in the hey-day of the community. While many of them are now deceased, they included Gerald Chilson, Ernie Perozzi, Howard Potter, Charlie Wanagitis, Carl Weed, Steve Potuck, Pat Dempsey, Lawrence Broschart, Leo McDonald

Kenan Fullerton, 12, with his dad, Don, from York, PA on his first day of hunting bagged this nice button buck. The Fullertons were hunting from a tree stand in Colley Township. *The Sullivan Review*, December 24, 2013.

and Al Dieffenbach. There may be others, but the names are another thing we didn't know enough to get on tape. Now, there's one more gone. So long, "Uncle Ed."
*The Sullivan Review*, June 18, 1981, p. 6.

## Bear Hunters Bag Wild Boar Near Dushore

A group of local bear hunters near Forksville had an unusual experience on Monday of bear season. While hunting in the mountains on State game lands six miles west of Dushore they encountered and shot a wild boar. The wild boar was downed by two hunters, Pete Fowler, a retired Montour County agent of Danville, and Elton Tait, assistant director of Penn State Extension Service of State College. The two are members of the Loyalsock Rod and Gun Club, which is made up of members of the Extension Service. Wild boar hunts are usually associated with Central Asia, North Africa and the forests of Europe. Although there isn't a season on wild boar in Pennsylvania, Sullivan County has had wild boar hunts for many years in conjunction with the autumn Bow Hunters' festival. The animals are brought in by truck from Georgia. This year 18 wild boars were released in the woods as 400 bowmen surrounded them in a large circle. Thirteen were killed by bowmen and five escaped, including the one shot by the two hunters above. The animal was in good condition with a full stomach of roots, grass and nuts. The imported wild boars are thought to be a cross between the Russian wild boar and the native "razorback" of southeastern United States. They are reared in the wild, trapped and sold to private preserves for wild boar hunts all over the country. One of these preserves, Le Van's, is located in northern Columbia County. One hundred dollars is charged for each boar killed. The two lucky hunters felt like kings or noblemen for a day. The head was brought in to the dining hall with great ceremony, and the hunters received special privileges and congratulations. The rest of the carcass is being processed at Ed Long's butcher shop in Monroeton. A wild boar feast will be held in the near future.
*The Sullivan Review*, December 12, 1968, p. 8.

## Johnny's Story of a Bear in the Kitchen

With bears on the move 24 hours a day, storing up fat for a long winter's nap, spooking dogs and surprising joggers and hikers, it's only natural that a man who drives around Sullivan County should see a bear now and then. Such is the experience of John Frystak, a service man for Commonwealth Telephone Company. Sighting wildlife is common for him. You may have heard this story, which he says is as true as the ring of the telephone at 3 a.m. John was sent to the Shrewsbury Township area of the county to install a new phone sometime ago. Arriving at the home, he knocked at the door. No answer; he knocked several times, still no answer, so he decided to try the door. There'd be a note inside with instructions, he figured. The door was unlocked. Upon opening the kitchen door, he saw a big bear cleaning up cookies, bread, and cake with sweeps of his furry front paw, quickly making a shambles of the kitchen. John stopped in his tracks, and as he tells it, "I didn't ask the bear where he wanted the phone. I left." Knowing a family with young children lived there, he stopped at the neighbor's, where he found the mother and her kids safe. Apparently they had gotten out as the bear came in. By the time everyone returned to the house the bear had gone. In his wake was a ruined kitchen, a refrigerator on its side, door open and empty of edibles. If you don't believe it, ask John.
*The Sullivan Review*, October 5, 1978, p. 7.

## Turkey Talk

We're into the season for turkeys, both wild and domestic, so a few comments about experiences with these birds might be timely. Going back 50 or so years, many of the small family farms in Sullivan County had two or three turkeys roaming the farm yard, subsisting on what they picked off the ground plus a combination of other grains used in the farming operation–corn, wheat, buckwheat or a mixture of these as found in chicken or cow feed. Things have changed. Not only are the small family farms gone, so have their turkeys. This year, 2009, we could not find one live turkey on a farm in Sullivan County. Among the reasons for the lack of the birds, besides the demise of subsistence farms, is the high cost of turkey feed. For the price of a hundredweight of turkey feed you could buy almost four oven-ready turkeys from the supermarket. They might not taste as good, but they don't have to be fed and watered for six months. Many years ago on a fall visit to the Ray O'Neil farm in Albany Township, I saw a nice big bronze tom walking around the barnyard. Ray and I agreed it would be just right for Thanksgiving or Christmas dinner. The big bird would gobble and fan his tail almost on demand. A year later, on another fall visit to the farm, the big bird was still there. I asked Ray why they didn't have it for last year's holiday. With an exclamation that could only come from a true Irishman, Ray said it was too big for the roaster and too big for the oven. So he was spared. The late Albert Exley of Mildred raised a variety of birds on his farm–peacocks, guineas, ducks, fancy chickens and wild turkeys. He also incubated turkey eggs. To comply with regulations the turkeys had to be blood tested yearly. Prior to incubating eggs the hen's blood had to be tested for pullorum disease (*Salmonella pullorum*, if the name hasn't

Darcy Sysock, 13, with her first turkey, a jake weighing in at a whopping 20-lbs. with a 10" beard. She got it at 6:50 a.m. in Cherry Township during a youth turkey hunt, and is seen here with her proud father, Tommy Sysock. *The Sullivan Review*, April 27, 2006, p. 5.

been changed). Each bird was caught and a sample was drawn from the big vein under the wing. If the bacterium is passed from hen to egg to chick, it can cause non-hatching eggs or sickly chicks and contaminate the incubator. After the blood was drawn, the bird would be released to fly up in a nearby tree. Another turkey story involves testing turkeys at the Joe Baldwin farm in Centermoreland, Wyoming County. Joe raised Empire Whites, a big, heavy bird desired by the hotel trade. A big tom, at maturity, would go 40 or 45 pounds. It was a day's work to bleed his flock, and at lunchtime Mrs. Baldwin would serve–what else–roast turkey sandwiches. None of this thin deli-style turkey, but slabs of white meat as thick as a thin steak, with home-made bread. They kept us alive for the afternoon session. In the late 1960s, when the Game Commission was trying to reestablish the wild turkey in state forests, several birds were released at Dutch Mountain. The program was successful, as wild turkeys proliferated and now are common. But before they were common, and early in our newspaper experience, a hunter came to The Sully office with a fine specimen he bagged "somewhere." We took his picture and put it in the paper. Later, we found out that he had purchased the wild turkey and wanted to be one of the first hunters to get a trophy and get his picture in the paper. So much for turkey talk.

*The Sullivan Review*, November 25, 2009, p. 2

Top: Dylan Higley bagged this 20-lb. gobbler with a 9" beard and 1 ¼" spurs during Youth Mentored Hunting day with his father, Mike Higley of Terry Township. *The Sullivan Review,* April 24, 2013, p. 1.

Bottom: Turkey hunters Bill Cole and John Hoodak with a friend at the Monument

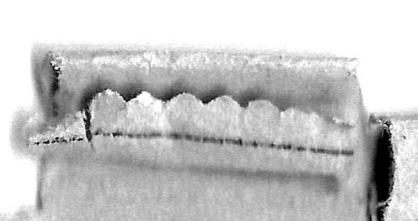

Tree farm, Overton Township. 2012

Colley Township farm, early fall in
the Endless Mountains

## Driving Away from Sullivan County and Coming Back

Last week we drove Route 487 over Dutch Mountain on our way to Wilkes-Barre. It was a hot Friday afternoon, becoming warmer as we descended Red Rock Mountain into the valley below. On the way down the mountain we saw that the road had newly painted white lines marking the edges of the road, yellow lines in the center, surely a welcome improvement for those who traverse the hill in foggy weather or at night. We send our thanks to the section foreman in charge. The visual advantage of lines will do much to prevent accidents on this stretch of road. Upon arrival in Wyoming Valley we were greeted by dusty construction sites, torn up roads, sewer construction, narrow streets, and holiday traffic. What isn't being re-constructed in the Wilkes-Barre-Kingston-Forty Fort area probably will be scheduled in the future. The flood of 1972 may have been unpleasant, but also a blessing. Returning to Sullivan County from the trip to Wyoming Valley was a joy. The temperature was pleasant, the roads much better, little traffic, and a great view of those ever-scenic Endless Mountains that surround us. Sullivan County is a real place to live!

*The Sullivan Review*, June 2, 1977, p. 11.

# Section 8

*Sullivan County Railroads and Doc's Rail Car*

van Revi

Union Station, Sonestown. Williamsport and North Branch train on standard gauge (left), narrow gauge Eaglesmere Railroad on right. Ca. 1905, when railroads drove the economy (Taber, 1969).

# Dushore Trestle Over Little Loyalsock Creek

From time to time we run across items of historical interest and try to make notes of them, but often they are lost or forgotten. At the Sullivan County Historical Museum in Laporte, there is an 1884 (or earlier) map of the Bernice Coal Fields, the original reason for building the railroad in this area. Recently, a friend sent clippings from the October 8, 1954 and March 31, 1955 editions of the *Towanda Daily Review*, with some interesting facts about the Dushore trestle that spanned the Little Loyalsock Creek gorge. The trestle, in effect, joined Dushore and Bernice, which were 8 1/2 rail miles apart. It was built around 1872 and was 333 feet in length, single track, with 26 frame spans and one steel span. It was about 47 feet above the streambed, and 33 feet above Route 87, which passed underneath the eastern end of the structure. Cost of construction in 1872 was $17,350. It was rebuilt in 1909. The salvage firm of Hyman and Michaels had contracted to pull up the rails from Bernice to Dushore, but when they got to the trestle, they sold it to Roscoe Burgess, a lumberman who used the timbers elsewhere. Throughout its length, the track had a slight curve. When the flood of 1928 damaged the footing of some of the piers, they were repaired with new concrete at a cost of $1,200. The line between Dushore and Bernice was known as the Bowman's Creek Branch. The Bernice coalfields were the northernmost semi-anthracite fields in the east; over the years of the Bowman's Creek Branch operation prior to World War I, 20,000 carloads of coal moved over the line each year. After the trestle was removed in 1955 Route 87 was widened to two lanes. Prior to this, the one lane underpass was a challenge to motorists, especially in the winter. Eventually Cherry Street, which met Route 87 just north of the trestle, was eliminated. The steel whistle sign that was placed in the middle of the trestle was recovered some years ago in the creek and is now in the Dushore Railroad Depot. Another note: one of the Shoemaker boys, a two year old, wandered off one winter day, and his mother couldn't locate him. Our neighbor, Gene Coyle, followed little footprints in the snow and caught up with Tom a quarter mile of the way across the trestle.

*The Sullivan Review*, July 13, 1995, p. 13.

High Bridge, Dushore, Pa.

Dushore Trestle, seen from the top, looking north. Old postcard mailed September 25, 1916 shows a planing mill on right,
coal storage on left. Mills and nearby buildings burned ca.
1937; the area is now the site of Dushore Agway.

Train at Satterfield Station, 1939

## Stories from Clyde Speary, Sr. and the History of County Railroads, 1892 – July 31, 1937

Even though railroads no longer run in Sullivan County, there remains plenty of historical interest in the 100 miles of track that once crossed the county, connecting the principal towns and providing local passenger and freight service. Of particular interest is the Williamsport and North Branch Railroad (W&NB), which ran from Hall's Station in Lycoming County to Satterfield in Cherry Township, Sullivan County. It operated between 1892 and July 31, 1937 and was built in at least two stages. For several years it ran only to Nordmont, serving the "acid factory," various lumber mills, the clothespin factory and other wood product factories at Sonestown. Some time later bonds in excess of two million dollars were sold to raise money to extend the line beyond Nordmont to Lake Mokoma, Laporte, Ringdale and the northerly terminus, Satterfield, named for John Satterfield, one of the railroad engineers. At Sonestown, the W&NB connected with the Eaglemere Railroad; most, if not all, of this history is detailed in the book *Muncy Valley Lifeline* written by Thomas Taber (1969) of Muncy and available at *The Sullivan Review*.

In 1982 George M. Hart, director of the Railroad Museum of Pennsylvania in Strasburg, Lancaster County, Greg Calaman, a Sullivan County High School student working independently on the history of Sullivan County railroads, and Doc Shoemaker conducted an interview with Clyde

Speary, Sr., the only surviving employee of the Williamsport and North Branch Railroad. Mr. Speary, who will be 83 on July 1, 1982, lives near Nordmont. He worked from 1925 through 1937 on the W&NB, the last nine as foreman of Section 8 of the line that included Satterfield, Bernice, Birch Creek, Ringdale, and partly around Karge Point toward Laporte. Following the official closing of the railroad in 1937, Mr. Speary supervised rail salvage. Most of the ties weren't worth salvage, having been purchased second hand from larger railroads. The rails were taken up beginning at Satterfield, where the W&NB connected with the Lehigh Valley Railroad, and proceeding toward Hall's Station. Among the facilities at Satterfield was a wye track, where an engine could be turned around, and headed in the opposite direction. Mr. Speary related that the W&NB track superintendent, Lewis Secules, couldn't understand why the distance between the rails on the wye was greater than elsewhere. If it weren't wider on the sharper (inside) curve the weight of the engines (around 45 tons) would cause the track to pull its spikes, possibly causing a derailment. When asked about water for the steam locomotives, Mr. Speary noted that in Ringdale, Dutchman's Run water was taken right out of the stream. Long Brook and Sonestown had water tanks, known as plugs; one night the tank at Long Brook ruptured but was never fixed, and today its foundation can still be seen along the right-of-way. The cold water of Dutchman's Run was thought to be, indirectly at least, the cause of the explosion of Locomotive No. 16 on Oct. 5, 1905. After extra cold water was run into a nearly empty boiler, Number 16 blew up a mile down the track from the Run, killing engineer David Davis and, a day later, the fireman.

Mr. Speary was asked if he remembered the names of other section foremen. He did: the Section 7 foreman at Laporte was Robert Hess; Section 6 at Sonestown, Carl Harvey; Section 5 at Glen Mawr, Charles Houseknecht; Section 4 at Picture Rocks, Harry Taylor; the Section 3 foreman at Hughesville was a man named Gansel. What a recall after 45 years, give or take a name or a section!

A train accident near Tivoli, known years ago as Dogtown, involved a family cow that was killed as it grazed along the tracks. The incident so enraged the cow's owner that he did something to the track that caused an engine to derail and upset. Cows or other livestock were always a problem for railroads traversing the rural countryside.

In concluding the interview, Mr. Speary told the story of the white pigeon. For some time, the Lehigh Valley ran a gas-electric car over the line between Towanda and Bernice. At Monroeton, a white pigeon would pick up with the engine and fly to Bernice. This went on for several months; at Bernice the pigeon would land on the crosshead of the engine and then ride back to Monroeton. No one could ever explain the motive of the bird. (Could it have been loco?)

## Snowplow on the Railroad

Is the world's climate getting warmer? Can we believe the climatologists who say it is? Looking back on 50 some years in Sullivan County it seems as if snowstorms aren't as wild as they once were, but who knows? Fifty years isn't a long time as far as weather is concerned. In one winter, between 1967 and 1970, we had a big snowstorm, several inches beyond a foot, at the time the Lehigh Valley Railroad was still coming in to Dushore. On this occasion, the railroad sent their plow to clear the tracks. The huge plow, mounted ahead of a caboose and pushed by the locomotive cleared the tracks between the station and the Agway siding. There was a time that PennDOT didn't start to plow until the snowstorm was over. Many times, the snow got so deep or drifts so big that the plows couldn't handle the job; they got stuck trying. Nowadays, plows go out ahead of the accumulation.
*The Sullivan Review*, March 3, 2005, p. 11.

## Story of the Rail Car

A history of the old railroad car that sits on a siding near the Dushore Depot was found in notes left in the estate of railroad historian George M. Hart, who died in April 2008. Mr. Hart, the first curator of the Railroad Museum of Pennsylvania in Strasburg, was well known for his knowledge of steam locomotives and his train photographs. These notes are from his long hand account of the car and how it came to Dushore.

The rail car, made by Harlan and Hollingsworth Corp. of Wilmington, DE, was built about 1910 as a full-length passenger coach for the Philadelphia and Reading Railway Co. The exterior finish was olive green and highly varnished,

Some figures on coal tonnage shipped over the W&NB were provided by archives at the State Bureau of Mines.

The Forksville Coal Co. shipped out of Laporte: 234 tons in 1934; 3,211 tons in 1935; 3,735 tons in 1936. No figures after this date. The Monahan Coal Co., Loyalsock field, shipped out of Laporte also: 8,961 tons in 1934; 2,000 tons in 1935. No figures after that date.

The Gunton Coal Co. at Bernice shipping out of Satterfield or Birch Creek: 44,289 tons in 1936; 17,393 tons in 1937; and 1,878 tons in 1938 (via LVRR).

Soft coal was stockpiled at Satterfield for use in the locomotives. This was apparently shipped from the western part of the state.
*The Sullivan Review*, March 18, 1982, p. 2.

the interior typical of day coaches at the time. Decorative features included paneled inlay, gold leaf striping on the ceiling, clearstory roofline windows of stained glass, and brass ceiling light fixtures. Coaches of this type were the Reading's first passenger coaches to have all steel under frames with open platforms instead of the closed vestibules now in use. The interior width of the car is 9 feet, length 72 feet coupler to coupler; it weighs 52 tons. In September 1929, the passenger seats were removed and the interior modified into three sections. It was renumbered 90882 for non-revenue wreck train service in the Philadelphia and New York divisions of the Reading Railroad and quartered at the Erie Avenue engine house in Philadelphia. The reconfigured interior included an office for the wreck master, 12 bunks, closets, kitchen cabinets, stove, refrigerator, water tank, mess hall and toilet facilities. The car was kept continuously in standby, fully equipped, supplied, ready to go, and attached to the tail of the wreck train. The wreck train, later called the service train, consisted of a "big hook," idler car, tool and supply car, the wreck master's car and a locomotive. A Baker water heater, kitchen and caboose stoves provided ample heat and hot water. The wreck

Steam engine at the Dushore Depot. Originally the Sullivan and Erie, then the State Line and Sullivan, and still later the Lehigh Valley Railroad ran four passenger trains a day through Dushore, as well as coal and freight trains.

Hillsgrove covered bridges, automobiles on left, railroad bridge on right. The bridge on the left was known as the "Bridge of Spooks;" it was demolished in the 1950s. Early 1900s image.

train was stationed at Erie Avenue until January 1965, when it was retired from service; the car was returned to Reading and purchased by private individuals. It remained in the hands of the railroad company until December 1965, and was to be shipped to Chalfont on the Doylestown Branch for storage at Hartzel's siding under an overhead coal shed. But the car was taken five miles farther than Doylestown, arriving January 4, 1966 at the former Atlantic Refining Auto-unloading platform. After four months it was returned to Chalfont, where it should have been left off in the first place. While there, the car was renumbered from Reading Company's 90882 to #26, to conform with the new owners' numbers. During January 1971, #26 was shipped on the State Line & Sullivan Branch of the Lehigh Valley Railroad via Lansdale, Bethlehem, Wilkes-Barre, and Towanda to Dushore, where it served as a place to stay for Dushore visitors. It had narrowly escaped a lightning strike and fire in August 1970 in the coal shed at Chalfont. Then it became landlocked in Dushore on June 22, 1972 following Hurricane Agnes, whose floodwaters weakened the bridges and abutments on the State Line & Sullivan Branch line. The bridges were never repaired between Dushore and Monro-

eton; in 1978 rails were removed, making Sullivan County only the second county in the Commonwealth without a railroad. Today, the car itself and track upon which it rests remain the last pieces of railroad equipment in the County. Shipped as freight from Doylestown to Dushore the charges were about $220. The original purchase price of the car in 1965 was $1050.

*The Sullivan Review*, August 19, 2009, p. 12.

## Electric Trolleys That Didn't Come to Mildred

On July 1, 1910, the Northern Electric Street Railway Company of Scranton was leased to a new corporation, the Scranton-Binghamton Railroad Company, for a period of 999 years. Principal officers of the old and the new companies were T.J. Foster, president (also president of the International Textbook Co.); F.W. Wollerton, vice-president; W.L. Connell, of Connell's Mines in Sullivan County, secretary-treasurer; and R.W. Day, superintendent of construction. As reported in the *Electric Railway Journal* of Feb. 25, 1911, and made available to *The Sullivan Review* by Edward H. Blossom of the Dushore Car Co., Inc., of Topton, PA, the Scranton-Binghamton Railroad Co. was to construct two additional lines: (1) to extend the Northern Electric System from Scranton to Binghamton via Montrose and (2) from Montrose to Wyalusing, via Camptown, with a proposed further extension to Mildred in Sullivan County. Great plans, but what happened? Northern Electric already had a line extending to Factoryville-LaPlume,

Doc's Rail Car, once Wreck Master's Car #26, on the siding in Dushore.
November 26, 1986.

and a six-mile branch from there to Lake Winola, a large private park in Wyoming County. Total mileage of Northern Electric was 20 miles, served by 14 passenger cars and four service cars. With expansion, profit possibilities looked great. The first extension of the line would begin at Factoryville and go to Binghamton, a 50-mile trip, to connect with the Binghamton system. The Montrose to Wyalusing branch was 30 miles via Camptown. When completed the entire system would embrace 110 miles and serve a population of 50,000 persons adjacent and tributary to the system, about 500 persons per mile. The Wyalusing branch would be a steam operation until business and finances could pay for electrification. A large summer trade to Montrose and Wyalusing was anticipated. The Scranton-Binghamton line would be shorter by 11 miles than the Delaware, Lackawanna and Western Railroad, which got to Montrose in a round about way from Alford, a junction some 10 miles east of Montrose on the main line of the DL&W. In addition, an extension of the line was proposed from Wyalusing to Mildred and Bernice. Dushore was not mentioned, probably because Mildred and Bernice were then more important as mining centers; also, Bernice native W.L. Connell was an officer of the railroad. The company obtained a 60-foot right-of-way, which would provide ample room for a double track plus high-tension transmission poles at a safe distance. Surveys were completed. The first two or three miles required rock cuts of up to 100 feet long, but the rest of the system would be easy to grade and construct. The first seven miles went from Factoryville to Nicholson. Standard gauge track of 75-pound (per three feet) T-rail would be used. Overhead wire would be similar to that used in Scranton. A 750 KW steam turbine located in the Dalton power station would supply the power, the technical details of which are insignificant now. The rolling stock was to be heavier, inter-urban type cars which had self-contained baggage and toilet facilities. Included in the baggage compartment would be space for dairy products, a lucrative source of revenue for the system because the area produced 5000 40-quart cans of milk per day, transported by horse and wagon to steam railroad sidings up to 20 miles away. The Scranton-Binghamton Railroad also planned a centrally located creamery to receive milk and produce high-grade dairy products that could then be transported to market more quickly. As a side note, the company's cars were painted Tuscan Red; they were washed twice a week with cold water and at four to six week intervals with No. 000 Emulsion of the Imperial Car Cleaner Co. After the dried 000 cleaner was rubbed off, Devoe's furniture polish was applied for a high gloss finish. The cost of the work: Imperial Cleaner, $1.05 per car; furniture polish, 1/2 quart at 75 cents per quart; 14 hours of labor at 15 cents per hour; total cost: $3.52 per car. To follow up on what happened, the line did get built to Montrose; it operated until the early 1930's. The extension to Binghamton and Wyalusing never got built, some say because of heavy (steam) railroad opposition and political influence. Then in the early 1930's, the company got in a rhubarb with the City of Scranton over taxes and street paving. The city tore up the trolley tracks leading to its center and the trolley ended at a terminal on the outskirts of Scranton, from which point passengers had to transfer to a city line. Well, now, the 999 years isn't yet up, but don't hold your breath. I don't think we'll hear a trolley bell in Mildred in the near future.

*The Sullivan Review*, February 5, 1981, p. 12.

## Ed Blossom's Cat's Tail

As last week's issue was sort of a memorial to Ed Blossom, who came to Dushore in 1974 to restore and reconstruct electric trolley cars, it is fitting to recall Ed's love for his cats. Cats were Ed's constant companions, both in Dushore and in Topton, PA, where he moved in 1977. At Topton, Ed had a handsome male cat with a beautiful bushy tail–the cat's pride and joy. Every night after dinner the cat would depart for the cornfield across the tracks from the Topton car shop for a night of hunting. Tracks of a busy Conrail (at that time), branch were well used, with fast freights passing night and day within 300 feet of the shop. One morning,

Rail Road Crossing sign, Headley Avenue, Dushore, January 13, 1977. The sign was taken down in 1978 when the rails were pulled; Doc restored it and put it in the Rail Car.

the cat returned for breakfast minus his beautiful tail, a puzzle, to say the least, because Ed loved his cat. What could have happened? The loss did not disturb the cat. Later that day, between trains, as Ed crossed the tracks on an afternoon walk, what did he find but the cat's tail, which had been neatly severed by a passing freight car wheel. How the cat escaped with only the loss of its tail will never be known. A miracle–the cat used one of its nine lives.
*The Sullivan Review*, April 28, 2005, p. 5.

# Section
# 9

*Recollections*

Bob with Noah and Jesse Phillips and their 4-H lambs. August 29, 2002.

# 4-H Days

Of all the activities available to young people in Sullivan County, none is more important than the many 4-H clubs [see above article on the Holstein cow affair, about Cherry Acres Barbara, daughter of Ron Hembury's first 4-H calf]. In a discussion Monday with David Kinsey, a youth coordinator for 4-H and other extension programs in northeastern counties, I recalled my experiences in 4-H in Luzerne County in 1937-38-39. I belonged to two clubs in Exeter

Bob and Ron Hembury and a 4-H heifer. September 29, 1978

Township, a 4-H Potato Club and a 4-H Capon Club. Our leader was then Luzerne County Agent Jimmy Hutchinson, and we met in the Exeter Township one-room school at Harding. Dues were ten cents. I found out that potatoes didn't do well in our rocky soil. After two seasons of hoeing, spraying and picking off potato bugs, my yield was a bushel or so of marble sized spuds. No prizes here. But I was more successful with capons, and as a reward I received a pocketknife from the Pittston Kiwanis Club, sponsor of my 4-H club. The little knife went to Penn State with me, through the war, through veterinary college and 30 years of practice; it still resides in my pocket. Having to its credit many jobs, from sharpening pencils to dehorning calves, it should be retired–but I'd be lost without it. One never knows where 4-H will go or lead, what it will influence. Where clubs are open, our young citizens should take full advantage of them. *The Sullivan Review*, September 13, 1979, p. 10.

Hembury family, left to right: Lynn, Ron, Emily, Tish, Willy, Ron, Bob.
June 1980, with 4-H cows

Green Swan Hotel, corner of Main Street at Route 220 in Dushore, and Sullivan County's only traffic light

## 1930s Prices at the Green Swan Hotel

Oh, for the good old days, at least when the prices were lower. A friend of ours showed us a menu from the Green Swan Hotel when Fred Benni owned it (in the late 1930's, perhaps). What a revelation to look at the cost of food at a time when a dollar was really worth a dollar. Featured on the extensive menu was T-Bone steak for $1.00; plate lunch, 35 cents; spaghetti and meat with bread and butter included, 35 cents; oyster stew, 25 cents. Beer drinkers will be pleased to hear that one bottle sold for 15 cents or two for a quarter. Rye highballs were 25 cents; old fashioned, 25 cents; whiskey sour, 25 cents; Tom Collins, 25 cents; Manhattan, 25 cents. Various omelets costs 25 cents and 35 cents; potato and fruit salad, 25 cents; tuna fish salad, 35 cents. How about a 15 cent hamburger; a 15 cent ham sandwich; a cold beef or pork sandwich for 15 cents; a 15 cent bacon sandwich; or a hot sandwich with gravy for 20 cents? With potatoes, this hot sandwich would cost you 5 cents extra. The breakfast menu included two fried eggs, two scrambled eggs or two poached eggs on toast for 25 cents. For 45 cents you could breakfast on two eggs and ham or two eggs and bacon. Toast included. Coffee included. The famous Dushore landmark is still operating under the ownership of John and Peggy Hoodak. Fred and Mae Benni sold the restaurant to Ralph "Shorty" and Celia Obert; then it was owned by Harold and June Kitchen, who sold it to Ted and Mary Czygier. Next owners were Joe and Ellie Sweeney; following them the Green Swan was owned and operated by Harold and Claire Boyer, then Chet

and Theresa Gleockler, then the present owners, John and Peggy Hoodak. While owners changed, so did prices. But that's the nature of things. Located on the northwest corner of the intersection of Route 220 and Route 87, the Green Swan Hotel was torn down around 1999-2000. The hotel's sign was a rendition of a swan made of tin and painted green; it disappeared sometime during John Hoodak's ownership.

*The Sullivan Review*, September 27, 1979, p. 14.

## Scrapbook Findings

One hundred years ago, in the early 1900s, the end of summer was a time to harvest whatever the home garden had in excess and preserve its goodness for the coming winter. Housewives brought out recipes–handwritten notes or cut outs from a magazine or newspaper–handed down by previous generations and kept in a scrapbook. In one such scrapbook, an old seed catalog was pasted full of recipes for a concoction known as "chili sauce;" some of the variations of the recipe follow. No recipe was needed for the paste, made of flour and water.

Aunt Rettie's chili sauce: 24 ripe tomatoes; 4 sweet peppers; 5 good sized onions; 3 Tbsp salt; 1 scant cup of brown sugar; 1 1/2 cups of vinegar; celery; 1 tsp each of cinnamon, cloves, allspice, and black pepper. Then boil together for 1 hour; should make 11 1/2 pints. Aunt Ida's version: 30 tomatoes; 8 stalks celery; 6 large onions; 4 tsp. salt; 3 cups of vinegar; 1 5/8 cups of sugar; 4 red peppers; 3 green peppers; 1 Tbsp. cloves; 1 Tbsp. allspice, 1 stick cinnamon; chop all the vegetables fine, tie spices in a bag, cook 2 hours and can hot. Aunt Dora's chili sauce: 5 quarts ripe tomatoes – chopped; 2 cups red peppers; 2 cups green peppers; 2 cups celery (all chopped); 1 1/2 cup onions; 3 Tbsp. salt; 1 cup sugar; 3 cups vinegar; 1 Tbsp. each allspice, cinnamon, cloves: combine all and simmer, then add vinegar and spices. Cook until as thick as you want it. Can it while hot. Aunt Martina's version: use same ingredients: 2 colanders of cut up tomatoes, drained; mixed vegetables, salt and sugar; heat through, then add 2 cups vinegar, spices, including 1/2 tsp. ginger and 1/2 cup brown sugar. Taste and adjust seasoning. Cook for a few hours; boil up small amounts to can, one jar at a time. So, choose your version. Goes best with home baked beans, boiled cabbage, baked potatoes, or anything you might want to spice up. I can now put the scrapbook away until the next time I clean my desk.

*The Sullivan Review*, September 3, 2012, p. 7.

## Playing in Governor Arthur H. James' Inaugural Parade, 1939

Readers of *The Sullivan Review* may be familiar with a long standing column, the "News in Review," which notes items that appeared in the paper many years ago. Last week's issue carried news items from February 1939, some 71 years ago. I was reading an issue on the microfilm and came across the following in the Bernice-Mildred news: "Among those attending the inauguration at Harrisburg were Betty Scott, Misses Minnie Evangelisti, Laura Panichi, Helen Hartford, Helen Reagan, Rose Hubiak and Dorothy Hembury." Like in the comic strips, a light bulb flashed in my mind. I was there, too. Newly elected the previous November, Governor Arthur H. James was a native of Plymouth in Luzerne County, of Welsh descent, and a Republican. Luzerne County was

Doc as a high school piccolo player in the John D. Stark Post 542 American Legion Band, 1939.

then mostly Republican, and it was a great honor to have a native son in the Governor's office. The county went all out to honor him. How did I happen to go?

In 1939 I was a senior at West Pittston High School, where my extra curricular activity was playing piccolo in the John D. Stark Post 542 American Legion Band from West Pittston. I remember two other classmates who played in the band, but most of the members were World War I veterans, then in their mid or late 40's. The band was hired to march in the Governor's parade in Harrisburg. Band members all belonged to the musicians' union, so the parade would be a "paid" job–$6.00. At the time, the band was active and well known throughout Wyoming Valley. The uniforms were replicas of those worn by the Royal Canadian Mounted Police–a scarlet red coat over black jodhpurs covered with black leather puttees. The hats were similar to those worn by today's Pennsylvania State Troopers. The band of about 40 members made a flashy display marching in any parade. Director of the band was Dr. Rufus M. Bierly, a practicing physician in West Pittston and a World War I veteran. On the day of the inauguration we got on the morning train at the DL&W station in West Pittston. Arriving in Harrisburg on a bleak, cold February day, we went to our assigned place in the parade formation and waited and waited and waited. It was cold and dark and the uniforms weren't that warm. The parade came and went, and there was time to go around the capitol to see some sights. Finally we were on our way home. I recall one incident when a member of a color guard tried unsuccessfully to take a flagpole through a revolving door into the Penn-Harris Hotel. I didn't have any trouble with the door–I was the piccolo player. Then I got to thinking, how do I remember all of this stuff? I was unable to locate any of the ten young ladies mentioned in the 1939 "News in Review" item. Perhaps some reader will recognize a name.

*The Sullivan Review*, February 10, 2010, p. 7.

[original title "Playing In a Parade"]

## Old Friends

As old friends pass on, I often remember some situation, sometimes humorous and sometimes not, in which we both were involved. I recall once being called to the Vernon Reibson farm in Elkland Township to treat a cow with milk fever. It was late on a summer afternoon and the cow was down in the pasture field, almost obscured by the hummocks. There was a thunderstorm coming out of the west, and by the time we reached the cow the storm, complete with lightning and wind, was imminent. There we were: I was giving an intravenous infusion to the cow and Vernon was holding the umbrella. Everyone survived.

*The Sullivan Review*, March 3, 1977, p. 10.

## Friends I Remember on Memorial Day

I have attended memorial services throughout Sullivan County for the last 24 years. It seems I always remember certain events and friends as I listen to the ceremonies, always with respect and emotion, for I am here and they are not, and the events are history. Among my friends, I remember Willie Franz, a high school and 4-H companion from Luzerne County. Willie went into the Navy at the outset of World War II and was on a PT boat in the Pacific when it was blown out of the water. He was a topnotch mechanic on a Model A Ford. His car was rigged so that when it was parked, by a flip of a switch, it was electrified and who ever grabbed the door handle got a shock. His car also had a cut out, a wire ring coming through the floor boards that could be pulled and in doing so, the exhaust bypassed the muffler. What noise. What speed. And then there was another trick the Tin Lizzie could do: it could backfire on command. Aside from mechanical ability, Willie was a 4-Her. We raised potatoes for our project. They turned out to be marbles, but we had fun. Another friend I recall was

my roommate at Penn State-Alexander McCausland Mitchell, a big, tall blond kid from Glenolden, PA. Mitch hit the beach at Anzio and never got off. I also remember playing in Sutton's G.A.R. Band in Wyoming, parading through the cemetery to the bandstand on Memorial Day. How the people turned out to see the parade, led by Pennsylvania State Troopers on horseback. And, now I also remember those who don't have anything to remember, those who go through the cemetery, stealing the flags and bronze markers from the veteran's graves, the wrought iron flower urns from the graves of those who have passed on. Other things that pass through my mind as I listen to the band and the speakers include a field stone marker at a soldier's grave on Dutch Mountain.

*The Sullivan Review*, May 31, 1990, p. 7. [original title, "I remember"]

## Remembering Bob Lambert (1922 – 1995)

In Father McLaughlin's homily at Bob Lambert's funeral mass last Monday, he said the only thing Bob never did was sell huckleberries under the traffic light at Dushore, and that all his accomplishments were, in some way, secondary to his faith that any task could be accomplished. Who else but Bob Lambert could overcome the devastating handicap of blindness and do the things he did? Who else could get up at 5 a.m., grab a bowl of Post Toasties, walk downtown alone with his cane, open the garage at 6 a.m. and begin pumping gas? I have often thought that Bob Lambert had a day's work done before most of us got up. An unbelieving *Wilkes-Barre Times Leader* editor called undertaker Dean Homer last Friday and asked how one man could have done so many things. Dean replied that what was in the obituary was only part of what Bob did. All

true. Twenty-nine years ago, in 1966, when we were considering the purchase of *The Sullivan Review*, Bob Lambert and I put figures on paper, explored the ins and outs of publishing a community weekly. The conclusion was to do it, and Bob said he'd put an ad in every week. That he did, and has done so ever since. I can honestly say, that without Bob Lambert, I probably wouldn't be writing this today. It's not easy; the excitement of publishing is soon tempered when the editor has to bid farewell to a close friend, and put words to the feeling. Some things not in Bob's obituary should be remembered. As a regular Red Cross Bloodmobile donor, Bob holds a record: 11 gallons and six pints. As a dedicated County citizen, he reactivated the Chamber of Commerce and picked up the salary of the executive director until the organization could manage on its own. He founded and financially supported the Sullivan County United Fund drive. As program chairman of the Dushore Lions Club, he saw that there was never a meeting without a program. With the loss of sight, Bob's other senses were enhanced. He could ride in a car and pinpoint a noise or a rattle. He could feel the outside of a car and evaluate its condition. He could sense the presence of others in a room, and cross the street unassisted. Bob was a whiz at mental math, a skill taught in the one room school in Pleasant Valley. He didn't need a computer to calculate the sales tax on a retail sale, even when totals were odd amounts. He had in his memory dozens of phone numbers and could recall a voice and put a name to it. Bob left his family and all of us an irreplaceable gift and lifelong talent. I can picture him now at the Ford Garage in the sky, pumping gas, calculating the gallons by the bell on the pump, talking to a voice he's never seen and recalling the voice's phone number, 928-8184.

*The Sullivan Review*, September 7, 1995, p. 9. [original title "Remembering"]

## Nightlife in Overton

You might wonder why a small village in the largest township of Bradford County would even exist, much less have a historical past highlighted by its nightlife. Back in the 1850's Overton Township was founded by taking parts of several contiguous townships. Originally called Danville, the name was changed to Overton in honor of attorney Edward Overton. Irishmen and Germans who had worked on the North Branch Canal populated the village and surrounding small farms, although the area was not near the Susquehanna River and its canal. They stayed and eked out a livelihood on virgin forestlands. One settler was William Cahill, who came to Overton in 1853, cleared his land and lived until 1893. A story tells of his 32 mile-round trips to Towanda with his team of oxen. The Cahill Mountain is his legacy. What kept the town going was that Overton became a "pit stop," something like a modern truck stop along an interstate highway, for travelers and drummers on the way to Towanda, usually a two-day trek with horse and wagon. In Overton there was always a hotel, the first run by a Daniel Heverly from 1851 to 1860 in his store. Overton House was built in 1868 and operated about six years until it burned to the ground. James J. Hannon built a third hotel, the Hannon Hotel, on the same site in 1877. It continued to operate into the 1950's and was a welcome refuge for weary travelers seeking food, water and rest. In addition, Overton was like a big "convenience store," boasting numerous business enterprises: Osthaus and Co., general merchandise; a creamery operated by E. Franke and Son; a machine shop and manufacturing facility run by E.G. Musselman; two blacksmiths, William Bird and G.L. Rinebold; a shoemaker shop run by George Bower; a barber, J.B. Smith; and a physician, Dr. A.J. Bird–so much activity

that the town fathers thought of incorporating a borough. Three churches were founded: Methodist in 1823, German Reform Congregation in 1830, and Roman Catholic, St. Francis Xavier, in 1888. Travelers and at least two dozen small farms producing milk, cream, potatoes and other vegetables kept the business community and hotels alive. The foregoing is taken from historical publications by Chester Heverly and H.C. Bradsby, available in libraries and online. But we haven't gotten to the nightlife part of the story yet. In the 1950's, Maggie Hannon ran the Hannon Hotel and her sister was the cook. They catered to thirsty farmers who walked in or were brought by relatives. Food was available, 50 cents for all you could eat, according to Stanley Hottenstein. After a hard day on a farm or in the woods, Maggie Hannon's Hotel was the place to go. One clear, cold October night in the 1950's I received a call to attend a sick cow at the Francis Litzelman farm, almost diagonally across the road from Maggie's. Can't recall the problem, but after I left the barn I went into the hotel. Three men at the bar wondered who was that kid who came in the door in slush boots, coveralls and a baseball cap. I stepped up to the bar and asked John Leljedal, the bartender, for a Scotch and soda. He looked over the top shelf and got a bottle of Johnnie Walker, poured a shot glass full and waited for me to order a beer chaser. I had asked for soda. He went into the kitchen and returned in a few minutes with a box of Arm and Hammer. I don't recall the outcome, but I know I didn't drink the Scotch with a beer chaser. Now all the activity in Overton is gone; automobiles, the railroad and telephones turned the village into a wide place in the road. The Hannon Hotel is now a private residence; the Catholic Church is gone except for its graveyard. Most of the little farms listed below are history, but family members still operate a few on a larger scale. With the help of Mary Lambert, who lives near Overton, a list of the long gone farms within a mile or so of the town includes Francis Litzelman, Elmer Gloeckler, Walter Sherman, Otis Houseknecht, Leon Fetherbay, Herbert Dibble, George Bahl, Lloyd Streby, Bernard Broschart, Luther Treaster, Paul Marshall, Lawerence Keaton, Arthur Hottenstein, Frances B. Kelly, John Litzelman and Oscar Shrimp. Among those still operating are William Lambert, Michael Rouse, Jim Warburton, Dennis and David Hottenstein and Joe Cullen (Tom Burke). Sons and grandsons of the earlier generations keep the farms in business, but there aren't many old timers around to tell the stories of Overton and its nightlife.
*The Sullivan Review*, November 10, 2010, p. 18.

## Once Upon a Time, Old Time Veterinarians Reminisce

Northeastern Pennsylvania "Old Time Vets" and some not so old met at the Wyalusing Hotel on October 11th for their annual get-together luncheon and story telling afternoon. In addition to the "old timers" who were in practice when dozens of small dairy herds abounded, two recent graduates interested in farm animal practice were in attendance. Dr. Megan Tiffany, VMD, of Athens, a 2012 graduate of the University of Pennsylvania School of Veterinary Medicine (Penn Vet) has opened a mobile farm animal practice from her home. Dr. Mike Sheruda of Dalton and Narrowsburg, NY, a 2011 graduate of Penn Vet, is associated with a farm practice in Narrowsburg. Most of the others attending have retired from active practice, except Dr. Bryan Lee who has a dairy practice in Tunkhannock, Dr. T.W. Shoemaker, who has a companion animal clinic in Dushore, and Dr. Walter North, who specializes in bovine embryology. The old timers recalled their years of services rendered to small family subsistence farms that stressed rural life more than financial security. Treating farm animals, a small herd of 10 or 12 milk cows, maybe a team of horses, a pig or two, a pet lamb or a flock of sheep, was all in a day's work. Nothing really scheduled except, perhaps, a herd test for tuberculosis. The vets were part of the farm family, sharing concerns with young and old. Sometimes payment included a piece of apple pie or some freshly dug carrots. The cars driven by the vets contained medicines or equipment needed for the day's calls. Bad weather? Snow? Mud? All were part of the job. I always carried an axe, a buck saw, a log chain and a bumper jack (remember cars with bumpers?) just in case there was a tree down across the road or a sinkhole to bury a wheel. Among those attending was Dr. Jim Watson, now 93, with a sharp memory of his days in practice. He wrote a book called *A Country Veterinarian Reminisces* with dozens of his stories, including farm calls with a helicopter. He started out as a registered nurse during World War II in New York City, where he met his future wife, also a nurse. A story about each practitioner at the luncheon would more than fill three books, if only there was time to write the stories. So much has changed in the practice of veterinary medicine that much of what was taught 60 years ago is history. The little farms are all gone. The big farms are managed with sophistication that's hard to believe. The teaching of physical diagnosis of years ago has been updated or supplemented with evidence-based diagnosis. Practices have become more specialized. A paragraph from Dr. Watson's book summarizes the old timers' experience: "I'm thankful I practiced in the years that I did. Things have changed so much with farming, the new regulations, new medicines, new treatments and, above all, the mindset of people in general. Back then a handshake was all you needed to do business, life was slower paced and relationships were closer between doctors and clients." Today it's computers, ultra sounds, digital X-Rays, blood chemistry analyzers, office managers, cell phones and fancy medicines. No more colored water tonics, tire chains in the trunk or made-in-the-office medicines. It's a new age, so let's keep looking ahead.

*The Sullivan Review*, October 24, 2012, p. 9. (original title, "Once upon a time")

## Thanksgiving Thoughts

One of my bosses directed me to write something about giving thanks at this Thanksgiving time of the year. Note, I said "bosses," to each of whom I must say thanks for keeping me busy and out of trouble. I should start by thanking my elementary school teacher who taught me cursive writing, what I'm doing now. The Palmer Method has come in handy all these years. It's something that isn't taught nowadays. Thanks to word processors, kids don't have to write longhand, and don't have the skill. But don't blame kids; I know doctors and PhD's whose handwriting would baffle an Egyptologist. The keyboard and the Internet have finished the fine art of cursive communication. Moving on with thanks, we should perhaps thank everything we complain about, like the high cost of taxes, fuel, basic necessities and even non-essentials. Where would we be without the infrastructures that provide us with water, sewage, electricity, roads and other municipal services? Thankfully, we have them. Ninety or 100 years ago there were no decent roads, water came from a dug well, there was no electricity. There was wood to cut or coal to break with a sledge. Survival was a thing to be thankful for, and still is in a way, for those less fortunate. Can you picture a family in rural Sullivan County in 1910? Be thankful that a trip to a cold, smelly outhouse isn't necessary; that there's not a flock of chickens on the back porch; that you don't have to go out to the barn and milk a cow by hand, or worry about the kids getting sick with a doctor a half day's trip away. These people were thankful that a winter's supply of food–potatoes, carrots, apples, cabbage–was stored in the root cellar; that the horse didn't go lame and a wheel didn't fall off the wagon. We are thankful that we can drive to the grocery store, get five pounds of potatoes, flour or sugar at any time, in any season. Thankful we are who are in good health, and, if not, that medical services and medicine are readily available. Going back to 1910 what were the options? A teaspoon of baking soda in a cup of warm water or a spoonful of honey for what ails you. We can thank all our pluses to garner more votes than our complaints. Just don't eat too much turkey on Thanksgiving Day, be of goodwill and give thanks you got out of bed this morning.

*The Sullivan Review*, November 21, 2007, p. 18.

Mary Richlin's tom turkey strutting for the hens. November 24, 1982.

## Christmas Memories from the 1920s and 1930s

"'Twas the night before Christmas" will be repeated many times over the holiday season, while children of all ages wonder at the sights of St. Nicholas, his reindeer and sleigh full of toys. Present day children can't imagine going 'cross country in an open sleigh to grandma's house, bundled up in blankets with a hot stone for a foot warmer. In the 1820's, Clement Clarke Moore, the poem's author and a professor of religion at a theological seminary in New York City, could not have foreseen transportation today as he wrote the famous poem for his children's Christmas. I recall some by-gone Christmas holidays from childhood. The stockings were hung from the mantle of the fireplace, about the only source of heat in the house except the old Pittston coal stove in the kitchen. There was always a lunch left for Santa, because by the time he arrived at our house out in the country, he would be hungry. He usually filled our stockings with English walnuts, hazelnuts, an orange–only available at holiday time then–a popcorn ball and some little toys, a new toothbrush, maybe a pair of shoelaces, and hard Christmas candies. One Christmas morning we found an electric train assembled by Santa around the base of the tree. Another time he left a toolbox with tools, some of which I still have–the try square, for one, a template for measuring whether an angle is square. Some years a standard gauge Lionel train went around Dad's hardware store above the shelves and showcases. The coaches and Pullmans were equipped with inside lights, which always attracted attention. The track bed was a wide board supported by posts; the layout was protected by short, white dowel guardrails should the train jump the track. One year Santa came to town on the train; he boarded the afternoon DL&W passenger train at West Pittston and rode it southbound to Wyoming, where he was met by crowds of people on flat cars throwing paper streamers as he emerged from the passenger coach. On hand were a band, a number of floats built on those new-fangled flat bed trucks, and some old Packard and Pierce Arrow sedans, the real status symbols of the time. Santa was the star of a grand parade to my father's hardware store, where he received written and oral lists from the children in town. The hardware store was decorated for the holidays with displays of sporting goods, toys, outdoor clothing (the original

Winter tree with snow

Snowy day along the Williamsport & North Branch
railroad grade, looking west. A tank once stood
here, holding water from Dutchman Run to supply
steam locomotives. January 26, 1995.

Woolrich red and black plaid woolen coats), sleds, trains, skates and Winchester tools and rifles. The whole event was recorded on film by Wyoming photographer Charles Tracy and later shown at the Saturday matinee at Pete Marino's Wyoming Theatre. This was all before the Great Depression began to shut down the economy. Even shopping malls would be hard pressed to put on such a show today. In those days, the holidays seemed to be a lot of fun for everyone, not so commercial. We were glad for a yearly batch of popcorn balls, nuts and oranges in our stockings, along with little things we really needed, nothing fancy. If you weren't a good kid there was the possibility you'd get a few lumps of coal in the toe. Later, Mom would have that famous Christmas dinner – a freshly killed turkey, mashed potatoes, Hubbard squash, scalloped oysters, and condiments of celery, perhaps olives, homemade sour pickles. Topping it all off, steamed plum pudding with hot, thick, sweet, lemon sauce. No use rambling anymore, I have to do some Christmas shopping. Best wishes to all from the "Satterfield Flyer."

*The Sullivan Review*, December 24, 1981, p. 2; December 22, 2005, p. 16; and Dec 24, 2013 p, 2.

## Weather and Sounds

Last Sunday morning the air was cold, clear and very quiet, no noise of any kind when I stepped out of the office–no wind, no traffic, no jets, no birds. At that instant I thought I heard a siren. I listened and heard it again. Sure enough, it was coming from somewhere north of town. I asked the person who was with me if New Albany had a siren for its fire alarm. They do. A phone call to New Albany confirmed what I heard: an alarm had been sounded. What was unusual was that the sound carried so well so far, about seven miles. I recalled then that whistles on steam locomotives or factories were often more evident just before a storm, especially in winter when a snowfall was imminent. As it happened, Monday we did have rain and it might have been snow had it been colder. Once, many years ago, I stood at Saxe's old barn, east of Dushore along Route 87, and distinctly heard the rumble of a freight train on the Lehigh Valley railroad, located on the far side of the Susquehanna River at least 10 miles off. There were times, too, that the steam whistle on Harrington's Creamery in Dushore could be heard 8 or 10 miles distant. Most often, these sounds were followed by stormy weather the next day. Has anyone else noticed such sounds coming from a long distance?

*The Sullivan Review*, November 12, 1981, p. 12.

Whitetail deer yarding in the distance, Ron
Hembury farm. March 17, 1994

## Whitetail Deer Yarding in the Moonlight

"The moon on the crest of the new fallen snow gave a lus-
ter of midday to objects below." This line from the famous
poem about the night before Christmas was recalled last
Thursday night about midnight upon hearing the following
story from Bill Frazier of Muncy Valley. On a clear, cold
moonlit night earlier in the week, as Bill was going to the
barn around 10:30 p.m., he glanced out across his corn
field. In the moonlight he could see several deer standing
in the field, so he got binoculars and observed them. As
they stood, the deer were pawing the ground, loosening
tidbits of corn from the stubble. Some were just reclining
in the snow, eating from the ground. Relaxing. The most
amazing thing was the number of deer he counted–a total
of 55. That is a big herd to be yarding at this time of the
year. Our weather prophets might equate this to more snow,
more cold weather (which we have had), an early spring,
or it might be just a popular nightspot for whitetails to get
together. After all, humans flock to nightspots–Stumble
Inn, Birch Creek, Gardner's, Grey Fox, as examples. They
eat, relax and paw at the dance floor.
*The Sullivan Review*, February 2, 1984, p. 6.

Winter along a creek

# Acknowledgments

We greatly appreciate access to *The Sullivan Review* archives by publishers John A. and Christine S. Shoemaker and the assistance of staff members Rose Gumble, Tammy Bird, Katie Shoemaker, and former staff member Bob Phillips. We thank Tom Shoemaker, DVM, of Sunset Beach, NC, who served as a reviewer and wrote the Forward, and Leayn Stockdill, of Laporte, PA, reviewer and copyeditor. Logistical support was provided by Sarah Jensen, James G. Smith, and Jerry and Amy Plasto of the Hotel Harrington, Dushore.

Images are largely by T.W. Shoemaker or from his postcard collection, also by Bob McGuire, Brittany Serafini, and others of *The Sullivan Review* staff. Cover photography, images of Doc at a horse clinic and the Dr. Daniels cabinet are by Jamie Smith. Wyoming, PA, *www.twshoemakerart.com*. Railroad images from the 1930s and 1940s are by George M. Hart, former Director of the Railroad Museum of Pennsylvania at Strasburg, Lancaster County. Others who contributed photographs include Peter Shoemaker, Jackson G. Terry, and Martina Denman. Note that until about 2003 all photography for the newspaper was shot in black and white. Many of the negatives were retained, filed by topic and publication date in The Sully archives.

## Additional sources of information:

Eagles Mere Historical Society, Barbara James; Lycoming County Historical Society, Williamsport; Osterhout Free Library, Wilkes-Barre, Elaine Stefanko; the Sullivan County Historical Society, Melly Norton, who provided the image of the Harrington and Co. Creamery. Elizabeth W. Adler, Cupertino Hills, CA, consulted on the early development of the book, and Rosalind T. Helz, Chevy Chase, MD assisted with selected images. We especially appreciate the guidance of our designer, Sara Moore, who mentored us on the fine points of bringing an idea to publication.

Book cover and layout design by Sara Moore | *www.saramooredesigns.com*
Printed by: Payne Printery | *www.payneinc.net*

Additional copies are available from *The Sullivan Review*, Dushore, PA, *www.thesullivanreview.com*

# References cited

Many authors, 1954, *Sullivan County Industries, Then and Now* (1954). Published by the Endicott Printing Company, Endicott, NY; reprinted 1993 by the Sullivan County Historical Society at *The Sullivan Review* Press, Dushore, PA, 58 pp.

Margargel, Myrtle, 1955, *Historical Hodge-Podge: past and present pioneer makers of Sullivan County history. Owego, NY:* Tioga Publishing Company.

Streby, George and Streby, Clara A., 1903 [reprinted 2001 by *The Sullivan Review* Print Shop], *History of Cherry Township. Dushore, PA. Sullivan Gazette* Print, 58 pp.

Taber, Thomas T., III, 1969, *Muncy Valley Lifeline.* Published by Muncy Historical Society, Muncy, PA, 76 pp.

Taber, Thomas T., III, 1974, *Tanbark, Alcohol, and Lumber*, Book 10, published by Lycoming County Historical Society, Williamsport, PA, 99 pp.

The Hermit of the Kahill, 1979, *Musings from the Mountain with the Hermit in Sullivan County,* illustrated with photographs of Sullivan County, Pennsylvania by *The Sullivan Review*, published by *The Sullivan Review*, Dushore, PA, 81 pp.

Wallace, P.A.W., 1965, [reprinted 1998] *Indian paths of Pennsylvania*, Pennsylvania Historical and Museum Commission, Harrisburg, PA 1998, [1965 ISBN 0-911124-39-9] 227 pp.

Watson, Dr. James P., 2009, *A Country Veterinarian Reminisces*, privately published, 228 pp.

White Charolais beef cattle relaxing in a pasture, Dwight Lewis farm, Hillsgrove, 1969. The breed was brought to the US and Mexico from France in 1934 and came north in the 1960s. Crossed with breeds such as Angus and Hereford they produced more red meat and less fat (Wikipedia, November 15, 2014).

# Index